PRAISE
MARKETING AUTOMATION UNLEASHED

"Marketing automation isn't just a technology, it's a new way of marketing. In this book, Casey lays out a great roadmap to help you understand both aspects of this new frontier in an easy and straightforward way."

—Mathew Sweezey, principal of marketing insights, Salesforce; author of *The Context Marketing Revolution*

"Casey shares the marketing strategy that works and keeps it connected to the technology with clear, actionable advice."

—Nate Skinner, VP of product marketing, Salesforce Pardot

"It's an adventure out there. Marketers would do well to rope in with Casey and his strategic approach to better marketing."

—Sangram Vajre, chief evangelist & cofounder, Terminus: Account-Based Marketing

"Casey provides a pathway for marketers to break free of the tactical hamster wheel and think big picture MarTech strategy."

—Darryl Praill, CMO, VanillaSoft

"Converging technology has ushered in the melding of sales and marketing teams. Everyone connected to revenue generation should read this book."

—Tracy Eiler, CMO, InsideView; coauthor of *Aligned to Achieve*

MARKETING AUTOMATION UNLEASHED

MARKETING AUTOMATION UNLEASHED

The Strategic Path to B2B Growth

CASEY CHESHIRE

Advantage®

Published by Advantage, Charleston, South Carolina.
Member of Advantage Media Group.

Printed in the United States of America.

10 9 8 7 6 5 4 3 2 1

ISBN: 978-1-59932-738-9
LCCN: 2019919168

Cover and layout design by David Taylor.

For Tina, Lizzy, & Jon

CONTENTS

THE GROWTH PHASE

ALIGNMENT PHASE

OPTIMIZATION PHASE

The Hard Corps Marketing Show is a podcast that I host, interviewing the top B2B marketing professionals. Marketing myths are dispelled and the experts share their stories, best practices, and career advice for marketers advancing in their journey.

Throughout this book, I will reference certain episodes that contributed ideas that I learned from all the different conversations. If you want to know more about a topic that is covered, I highly recommend you check out the expert episodes!

Whenever a podcast is referenced in the text, it will look like this.

https://www.hardcorpsmarketing.com/

The Hard Corps Marketing Show **can be found on the following apps:**

iTunes
Apple Podcast App
Google Play
Spotify
Stitcher
YouTube - Full video

Follow *The Hard Corps Marketing Show* **on:**

Twitter (@HCMarketingShow)
Facebook
LinkedIn

FOREWORD

A wise man once said, "A few years from now, we won't call it digital marketing; we'll just call it marketing."

For more than twenty years, marketers, myself included, have developed deep functional expertise in digital platforms for advertising, communications, and analysis. I was the digital guy, the one who understood how to take what was possible with search, or social media, or rules-driven email and deliver results. We drove new leads, new customers, and lots of new revenue. Digital made marketers tech heroes. Pundits declared that the CMO was becoming the new CIO (and in some cases had larger tech budgets to boot).

But the advent of advanced marketing tech didn't change the outcomes that businesses desire; it only created greater opportunities to drive them successfully at higher efficiency and lower cost. The core of marketing's mission—driving awareness, consideration, intent, and actions—has always remained the same. When digital was properly incorporated into the overall business strategy of an organization, it drove those outcomes in spades. Digital enabled us to reach more people with the right message at the right time to drive the right action—the same thing marketers have been doing for centuries, just at higher scale, lower cost, and better measured visibility.

More than ten years ago, Casey Cheshire and I worked together at Transparent Language building an online consumer business to help people learn foreign languages. We would have killed to have had access to the type of MarTech stacks and automation platforms that are available today. The things we did then that involved a lot of manual segmentation and hours of analysis would be *so* much easier to do today. But the most important thing we did was to understand our business objectives, devise strategies to drive those outcomes, and make sure our tools and programs delivered against that.

And that is what many marketers and businesspeople miss. The capabilities of the tech don't matter if they're not serving the outcomes the business needs. How many organizations start with the tools rather than the strategy? How many organizations spend millions of dollars implementing complex MarTech stacks and connecting data flows to them, only to treat these complex systems as overpaid ways to "blast" a list once a month, or once a week, or (heaven forbid) every day? How many marketers measure their effectiveness with campaign metrics vs. business metrics, open rates vs. revenue?

And that is what makes the notion of a marketing automation maturity model that focuses on driving strategic outcomes so interesting and so important. What Casey does with his team at Cheshire Impact goes well beyond platform implementation and integration. They help their clients to make real business impact (it's in the name!). And in doing so, they've learned a thing or two about how marketing automation can serve those ends and how organizations can use it to drive the most value. Casey shares that in this book and gives us a framework to inform our own thinking on driving that value.

At the end of the day, if our marketing automation is driving those high-level business outcomes, perhaps we've finally reached the point where we're no longer digital marketers, we're just marketers. And super-effective ones at that.

David Meiselman
CMO, ezCater

AN INTRODUCTION WORTH READING

This is a book about growth and opportunity. It's written by a marketer, for marketers, and it was inspired by my own challenging (and often uncharted) journey to fully utilize marketing automation technology.

The suite of tools in marketing automation platforms allows B2B marketers to capture, nurture, and automatically engage their buyers in new ways that only a decade ago might have been considered science fiction. **The goal of this book is to ensure that you have the strategies and the road map necessary to maximize your use of this game-changing technology**. This book is not a technical training manual, but rather a road map for what specific strategies should be adopted in order to maximize your use of marketing automation.

Unfortunately, while marketing automation isn't new, many organizations still have yet to transition away from their email-blasting tools. Worse, many who have invested in the new technology have failed to make the transition to the new strategy. We scratch the surface of adoption, and our gut tells us something is missing, even if we don't know to what extent.

It's one thing to acquire a tool; it's another to actually use it. We've done our own research specifically with marketing automation and have found that the vast majority of organizations use 30 percent or fewer of available features. In other words, we're investing serious money into powerful tools and not fully using them.

Why is this? For some, it's a simple case of poor training. They either haven't been shown the ways in which they can use this technology, or they have but failed to make the connection that marketing automation is a completely new way of doing marketing. If you want the growth results, it's not business as usual. You must adopt and adapt, and more and more, you need to do both, quickly.

If you want the growth results, it's not business as usual. You must adopt and adapt, and more and more, you need to do both, quickly.

Others are embracing the new strategies of marketing automation but find themselves face-to-face with a gigantic to-do list. Powerful tools like Pardot allow you to do almost anything you can imagine, and that kind of limitlessness often leads to busy marketers feeling overwhelmed by the number of choices they must make to pursue so many opportunities.

I know this overwhelming feeling of opportunity personally. My own journey with marketing automation started almost a decade ago, when I left a large organization to run marketing for a midsized company that was still operating on the old model. Leads were stalling, no one filled out the twelve-field form just to receive the newsletter, and the unlucky few that did were unfortunately greeted by a call from a sales rep the following day. The salesperson had been through this before and didn't really want to call. Naturally, the surprised "lead" didn't want to chat either—imagine that!

It's a familiar story at a lot of organizations, and the friction in the buying process is palpable. I sought out solutions for this disconnected marketing and sales process as soon as I started. That's when I first discovered marketing automation.

I went through an eye-opening implementation and hungrily adopted an entirely new way of doing marketing, supported by this new technology. The concepts made sense, and heck, what did we have to lose!

Fast-forward several months. Leads were dramatically up and continuing to rise. Our forms were dynamically adjusting to the person viewing them (like Harry Potter magic!), increasing conversion rates and resulting in new lead counts dramatically. Prospects then experienced a customized series of email nurtures that educated and informed them (not pitched them!).

By the time our sales team received a lead, they had experienced an interactive demo and had been exposed to a white paper on the theory and a case study on the real-world successes possible. I went from "the new marketing guy" to "Casey" and was regularly invited out to a sushi lunch—which, for the record, seems to be the universal sign for when a sales team really likes you.

Finally, and most importantly, I was able to point to specific marketing efforts that led directly to won deals and the resulting revenue. With a proven ROI, I was able to immediately quit the worse lead sources and double down on the winners!

Very organically, this *passion* for marketing automation spurred my decision to launch my own consulting company, Cheshire Impact, allowing me to focus specifically on helping organizations achieve the same success with their marketing automation. With a dedicated team of experienced marketers and an amazing partnership with Salesforce, we've now helped more than twenty-two hundred organizations (and growing) maximize their use of marketing automation.

A ROAD MAP FOR THE BOOK

Where do you fit into the spectrum of fully utilizing your marketing automation platform? Until recently, I've found it's an easier question to ask than to answer. Maturity models for marketing automation are surprisingly hard to find, and disappointingly, they tend to be feature-centric instead of examining the bigger picture outcome of delivering qualified leads to sales in an overall revenue generation metric.

I had developed my own model from working on these platforms myself as well as from the many onsite consulting sessions I held. But this learned knowledge needed to be distilled and clarified so that it could be utilized, even if I wasn't there in person to articulate it. With that goal in mind, my team and I created a strategic road map for maximizing marketing automation, one that includes ten milestones comprising individual marketing automation strategies, each adopted in order.

My team and I created a strategic road map for maximizing marketing automation, one that includes ten milestones comprising individual marketing automation strategies, each adopted in order.

We called this road map the *Cheshire Success Index*, or CSI for short. The CSI takes followers through ten strategies grouped together in four distinct phases in their deployment of marketing automation: **Foundational**, **Growth**, **Alignment**, and **Optimization**. Each chapter of this book covers a specific step within each of these phases.

In chapter 2, we'll take an assessment based on your current adoption of these CSI strategies and put an actual number to that gut feeling you may already have about where you're at.

Following the assessment, the remaining chapters of this book cover specific CSI elements. Each presents experiences to learn from, strategies to implement, and criteria for success at that particular step. Because the order is deliberate, the work done in the earliest chapters will build like a snowball, creating an avalanche of marketing by the time you've hit all ten at the book's conclusion.

The first three elements describe the steps in the *Foundational Phase*. This critical phase revolves around establishing rock-solid buyer personas and ideal buyer profiles, preparing your marketing data, and ensuring your ROI reporting is ready to capture the results of the future steps.

The next phase is where marketers get to unfurl their wings and truly be marketers. In the *Growth Phase*, I'll use two chapters to break down the concepts of gated content marketing and deploying customized nurture campaigns.

The third phase is the *Alignment Phase*, and the two chapters there revolve around the collaboration between marketing and sales.

The fourth and final phase, *Optimization*, encapsulates some of the most advanced and fun strategies available to marketers today through marketing automation, including value proposition testing, dynamically changing emails, landing pages that speak directly to the visitor, and advanced analytics.

Now that you're all caught up on the logistics, let's get to it!

We're going to kick this party off by learning the four key values to marketing automation. Understanding them sets the stage well as you start learning the road map to success.

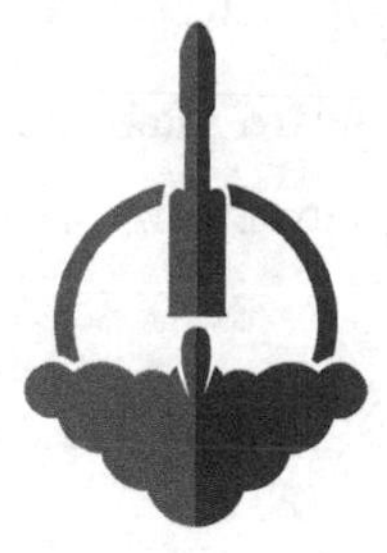

CHAPTER 1

FOUR LIFE-CHANGING WORDS

Since the invention of email in 1972, no B2B technology has had as much impact on the way we market and sell as marketing automation. From dynamically changing web forms and automated sequences of personalized emails to tracking marketing campaign ROI and a slew of extremely helpful features, there's no shortage of tools to experiment with and build. This can be a problem, too, as it leads to confusion and distraction from the most important strategies of marketing automation.

> *Capture, nurture, automate, report.* Four simple yet unbelievably magical words.

Capture, nurture, automate, report. Four simple yet unbelievably magical words. They are the core of what marketing automation can do to revolutionize an organization's marketing and set it on a course for amazing growth! Understanding these attributes of marketing automation gives you a great start toward maximizing your use of the technology and the context for implementing the more advanced strategies.

CAPTURE

There's an old joke about life that says you can only expect two things for certain: death and taxes. The grim reaper and Uncle Sam will always get their due. Everything else is negotiable. In marketing, you can add one more to that list. You can expect death, taxes, and sales asking for more leads.

Marketers are expected to generate consistent, prequalified, ready-to-purchase leads for their sales team to convert. The best marketers utilize lead generation sources to drive traffic to their website and other points in order to capture the information from the visitor. The act of gathering information from a visitor essentially creates a lead. Unless the form they're submitting is a request for sales contact, the leads are generally not ready to be sent over to sales.

When we help organizations implement marketing automation, one of the first things we do involves setting up forms. Different from the standard HTML form, marketing automation forms have dynamic abilities built into them. They remember the visitor, never ask the same question twice, and can insert additional questions if the previous ones have been answered.

So the first critical attribute of your marketing automation system is *capture*. (I'll discuss the best capture strategies for your marketing efforts a little later.)

NURTURE

Recently I was explaining the concept of nurturing to a conference room full of marketers. Projected on the wall was a picture from my wedding. I have my Marine Corps uniform on, and my wife looks beautiful in her wedding dress. I asked the audience, "How many dates did you go on with your significant other before you got engaged? Was it ten times, twenty, fifty? Was it one date? Did you even go on one date? Maybe it was in Vegas, right?"

Most people have many, many dates before they get engaged, but we tend to forget that lesson and treat it differently in the B2B world. We get really grimy and start moving way too fast with our marketing emails and unexpected phone calls from sales. Many companies send every person that completes a form right to a sales rep for follow-up. What is that? It's like asking someone to marry you on the first date!

Most leads aren't ready to get married when they first meet you either! Enter marketing automation-powered nurturing! What is nurturing? It's awesome. I like to say it's a sales tactic, because sales has been doing this for a long time. We train sales teams, and if they had unlimited time with their prospects, they'd be calling, providing value, caring for, and educating their prospects on an ongoing basis. So really what nurturing is, and what marketing automation allows us to do, is care at scale.

With apps like Pardot, you can program your nurturing campaigns based on your buyer's profile and persona. You can literally build it into the system, so you no longer have to manually send these emails out once a month or every week. You build them into the tool, and it sends them out on an ongoing basis.

The success of the nurturing process depends heavily on segmenting. Understanding who your buyers are and what their needs are will be critical to nurturing properly. I'll be diving into doing just that in the coming chapters.

AUTOMATE

I didn't get into marketing to spend three hours or more a day creating an email to send prospects, and I doubt anyone else did either. Unfortunately, though, that's the status quo, where we spend all month creating our monthly campaign, only to spend the next month doing the same thing. You feel like a hamster on a wheel, just with a laptop instead of cheese.

Before I started using marketing automation, I had actually asked for an additional marketer on the team because I was spending hours and hours doing tactical stuff. How can you possibly work *on* the business if you're working *in* it so much? How can you work on strategy if you're neck-deep in executing tactics day after day? It's impossible.

After I set up marketing automation, though, I felt like I had my own marketing team, because I could automate a lot of busy work and allow more time for optimization, testing, and creating impactful campaigns.

Automation is all about taking work out of your hands and enhancing the relevancy of the content to your marketing base.

Once you know what makes your prospect ready, all you have to do is set the criteria. Then the system is continually listening and watching. As soon as they are ready, the system takes them out of the nurturing campaign and moves them right to sales.

REPORT

Reporting is all about understanding what works so you can do more of it. You can't optimize unless you understand what works and what doesn't work. "Where do my revenue-driving leads come from?" That's the question that marketing automation can help you answer, and with a little bit of work up front, you can set yourself up for reporting that will help you move the needle.

When your marketing assets and activities are tied to campaigns that win viable prospects and revenue opportunities, you end up with a full circle lead that connects all of marketing's efforts with all of sales's efforts, so you can optimize your spending.

When your marketing assets and activities are tied to campaigns that win viable prospects and revenue opportunities, you end up with a full circle lead that connects all of marketing's efforts with all of sales's efforts, so you can optimize your spending. It sounds like magic, but it's all in a day's work with the use of marketing automation and customer relationship management (CRM) technology.

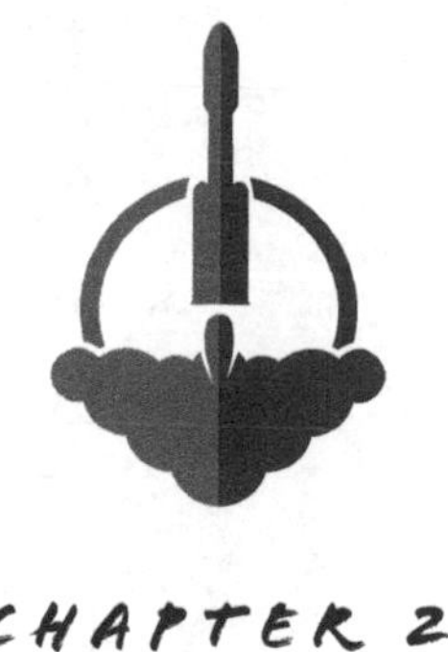

CHAPTER 2

VISION OF SUCCESS

There's a classic scene in the Disney movie *Alice in Wonderland*, with one of my favorite characters, the Cheshire Cat. He's a sly, striped, comically wise cat who just so happens to share the same last name with me. In this scene, a confused Alice is running down a path in the woods when she meets the Cheshire Cat, hanging out in his tree.

After seeing that she could go either right or left, Alice asks the cat, "Would you tell me, please, which way I ought to go from here?"

Cheshire Cat wisely replies, "That depends a good deal on where you want to get to."

"I don't much care where." Alice shrugs.

"Then it doesn't matter which way you go," Cheshire Cat tells her.

The same wisdom applies to just about everything in marketing too. You need to know where you're going in order to make the right steps to get there. If you don't care about where you're going, if you don't have a goal, then it doesn't matter what you do because you're

> You need to know where you're going in order to make the right steps to get there. If you don't care about where you're going, if you don't have a goal, then it doesn't matter what you do because you're just going around in circles in your own wonderland.

just going around in circles in your own wonderland.

Unfortunately, this ambiguity and confusion is all too common with marketing initiatives. The problem is further exacerbated by jumping right into a technology solution.

THE TECH TRAP

I remember buying a digital advertising platform early in my marketing career. It was supposed to help our organization do a better job of bidding and tracking our AdWords campaigns. We were spending over $100,000 a month on digital advertising, and our campaigns were terribly inefficient. The newly purchased SAAS platform had an impressive user experience with fancy buttons and slick performance charts. "This will be much more enjoyable to operate than analyzing rows of data in a spreadsheet!" we thought. Our team assumed that with minimal effort we could click some of these fancy buttons and the system would clean up the issues we had in our AdWords campaigns. That, unfortunately, ended up not being the case.

It did present data in beautiful visuals, but when it came to understanding why a campaign wasn't working, it wasn't helpful. Our campaigns still desperately needed optimization. I later came to understand from a PPC expert we hired to assist us that successful AdWords campaigns are all about identifying and addressing specific buyer intent. The tool was just there to help clarify things, but it didn't know the intent of each particular campaign. It was just there to be a guide, or help me do more of something, like spend *more* money on campaigns.

Despite the overwhelming amount of vendor marketing that promises the world, technology does not automatically solve everything. It can increase everything you're already doing, but it doesn't automatically create everything you need to do this. It only enhances it. Likewise, automation can only automate what you tell it. If you give it bad instructions, you're going to do a much better job of putting bad marketing in front of many more people than you did previously. Technology is not the cure-all. It's the amplification. It's the megaphone to make sure more people get the message.

There is a way to avoid this trap of believing that technology automatically solves all problems, and it centers around what you do before your first click in the new tool.

The story of Alice isn't so different from my own challenge with the technology purchase. Both of us were thinking tactically and neglected to confirm our overall destinations. This happens routinely in marketing departments around the world. We build various ads, landing pages, and emails and execute monthly campaigns. It can feel like a tactical hamster wheel that keeps us busy but without the satisfaction of ever reaching a destination.

The answer to never-ending tactical loops and execution missteps in marketing technology is to always start with a *strategy*. Next, mind your *process*, and customize it to your buyer's journey. Then and only then do you actually start executing the *technology*. Strategy. Process. Technology. If you follow this progression, you'll break out of the busywork of activity-focused marketing. The first step is to get clear on strategy.

STRATEGY

The most overused word in marketing is *strategy*. We hear it all the time, right? "We need to get strategic on this." I'll confess that I went through much of my early marketing career completely unsure of what this word actually meant beyond the notion that it was something important, and I don't think too many other people knew either.

> **Strategy:** A careful plan, or method, for achieving a particular goal, usually over a long period of time.

What's cool, though, is if you look up the word in the dictionary, it's actually way more practical than the abuse it gets in marketing circles. *Merriam-Webster*, via our friends at Google, defines strategy as, "A careful plan, or method, for achieving a particular goal, usually over a long period of time."

In other words, strategy is as simple as having a goal and creating a plan to achieve it.

There is nothing more clarifying than writing down a goal. Once it's written, you have a priority, and the very next task you work on should help you achieve it. The goal of this book is to give you the strategies you need to maximize your marketing automation and build a world-class B2B marketing program.

The second requirement to be strategic is creating an action-oriented plan to achieve your stated goal. We discussed marketing to be traditionally soft on goals, so it's no wonder that planning is also severely lacking in modern marketing organizations. One of the fastest ways to create a plan is to learn from someone who has already achieved the goal you're seeking. Similarly, this book is your plan, and the chapters are organized in the order they should be accomplished.

PROCESS

We once worked with a company who came to us with a real marketing tragedy. The previous year (before working with us) they had spent an additional million dollars on marketing. A million dollars! The numbers of leads they generated skyrocketed, but at the end of the year, they had zero growth in sales—no improvement whatsoever. It's as if that money vanished!

Understandably, they were feeling discouraged and needed serious help. We dove in, and what did we look at first? Strategy—but guess what? This company had one of the best strategies we had ever seen. They had a really good CMO and a killer strategy. They had the best technology too. What were they missing? Process.

They had generated a lot of leads with that extra million dollars, but unfortunately, because they didn't have a process mapped out, those leads were getting lost in various automations. More than thirty thousand leads were stuck in between the marketing software and the sales software. Marketing was pointing the finger at sales, saying, "We sent you these leads." Sales was saying, "We never got them." No one called any of those leads. At least a third of that million dollars was dying on the vine.

There were some other areas that weren't identified, too, like, "What happens when you recycle a lead? What happens when a lead isn't ready? Do you delete it? Do you send it back to marketing? Does marketing accept it?" None of these questions had been answered, and all of them were process questions.

Building a marketing process begins by mapping out the entire buyer's journey and then testing it as if you were the buyer. Ask yourself "what if" as many times as you need. When you get to a particular crossroads, ask yourself, "What happens if I go right in this process? What happens if I go left?" Test it out, see what happens to your buyer, and make sure you've thought of everything. "What happens if I send this lead to sales and they don't accept it? What happens if they do? What happens if after four calls, sales wants to send the lead back?" These are the kinds of questions you want to ask when you're auditing your marketing and sales process.

The need for process grows as the complexity of your marketing systems increase too. The larger the company, the larger the sales team, and the more important process becomes. You don't want to be that company that looked at strategy, looked at technology, but neglected the process.

TECHNOLOGY

Having conquered strategy and process, or at least having a plan for doing so, it's time to dive into building the technology. Once you've written goals for your buyers and mapped out a process for supporting them on their buyers' journey, you'll be surprised at how much clearer the next step is, like a weight off your shoulders. The remaining piece is to build the marketing automation required to get them from start to finish.

There will be some work to do, but it will be intentional and clear. You'll be building out different facets of marketing automation, and the fun part is that you can continue to customize as you go, tailoring the journey to the buyer. You also get to avoid the challenge of building something that you didn't actually need. Time and time again, we work with clients that have built something for the sake of building something. If you start with technology, that's what happens. If you start with strategy and then process, by the time you get to technology, that first step you take will be headed in the right direction.

When it comes to technology, let's remind ourselves, especially with marketing automation tools, that the point of automation is to make your life easier, not harder or more complicated. If you're finding yourself spending hours and hours and hours doing something that should be straightforward on technology, you're probably in the wrong system.

You want a system that gets out of the way. I didn't get into marketing to be messing around with tech. I wanted to create the copy, build the strategy, think about my buyer, and answer their questions to really help them out. That's why I got into marketing, and I'm guessing you had similar motivations. You need a system that enables you to do that while also staying out of your way.

The principles in the following chapters are universal for developing a world-class marketing automation system.

I personally prefer Pardot for marketing automation, and I can't promise I won't continue to crush on it periodically throughout this book, but you'll find that no matter what product you choose, the principles in the following chapters are universal for developing a world-class marketing automation system.

CSI: THE CHESHIRE SUCCESS INDEX

Successfully adopting marketing automation requires adopting new strategies for marketing. I meet a lot of people who have implemented new technology, but they haven't updated their strategy. It's not business as usual.

The challenge with adopting new strategies for marketing automation is that the systems can do so many amazing things and upgrade almost every aspect of your marketing program. How do you decide to do something when there are eighty thousand options? It's not like Alice trekking through Wonderland with two paths to choose from; here you've got eighty thousand different paths you can take! With that many options, the inevitable dilemma is, "What if I take the wrong path?" In response, many marketers stick to old strategies.

To date, we've worked with more than twenty-five hundred companies, from the *Fortune* 100s to small businesses like mine. We've had a chance to see what works, what doesn't work, and what the right order is for companies large and small. Everyone needs a clear path for fully utilizing their marketing automation system, so we created one.

The Cheshire Success Index (CSI) was created to help marketers gauge where they are in their use of marketing automation and provide them with the next steps necessary in order to reach their goal. It also gives an example of what a fully maximized system looks like.

We give everyone we meet a CSI assessment so we can help them improve their marketing and sales alignment and the use of their marketing and sales technology. This book is, essentially, a more in-depth CSI conversation, and you're going to find out your own CSI score in the next section.

By the time you finish the assessment, you're going to know where you are in the maturity of your marketing automation based on your score. You're going to understand what the next step is, which is represented by your lowest number. You will also know what a fully maximized tool looks like, as indicated by a perfect ten score.

We begin with a series of ten questions. These are somewhat tactical questions that relate to how you're using a feature in marketing automation, but the cool thing is that they also relate to marketing strategy. Each question builds on the next, so as you move forward with the completion of each step, the following steps have better results. This is not a "choose your own adventure" deal. We don't want you to skip ahead. This is a progression, and you'll see how following each step in order will make everything much more powerful.

How does this assessment work? Read each statement one by one. If you're fully doing everything the sentence describes, then give yourself a one (1) in that box. If you started doing it but you're only partially doing it, then give yourself a score of .5. Finally, if you're not doing the step at all, give yourself a zero.

This assessment is not about judgment, nor is it intended to make you feel bad if you have a low score. In fact, most of the people we initially give this assessment to end up with a score below 3.

The questions are designed to really make sure you're holding yourself to a high standard, so don't feel like you need to put a one (1) if you're not totally comfortable with that area. Think of the scoring as bookmarks. Anytime you put a zero or a partial credit, you're just reminding yourself where to come back to.

We typically conduct the CSI questions during phone calls with people or in person. While there is an assessment included in this book, we find that scores tend to be more accurate if the assessment is done with someone. That's because we ask follow-up questions to create a fuller picture of what's going on in your system. It's totally free to do that, and then you have someone talking you through each step.

There are four distinct phases in the CSI, and each one represents a different focus: Foundational, Growth, Alignment, and Optimization. Crossing phases marks a milestone that you should celebrate, which we do with our clients. It's not uncommon for our clients to receive some goodies in the mail if they cross a phase threshold.

Okay, now it's your turn. You can either take the CSI on the next page, or email **CSI@cheshireimpact.com** to schedule a CSI assessment over the phone with one of our strategists.

The remainder of this book will walk you through each CSI step, one by one, sharing successful strategies to help you maximize your system! (Cue the rock star music!)

CHAPTER TOOLS

CSI: Cheshire Success Index for Marketing Automation

Answer each of the following questions. If the answer is completely "yes," put a 1 in the Your Answer column. If you've started or are incomplete with a step, give yourself a .5 to remind yourself to come back to the strategy. The corresponding marketing automation strategy is noted after the question.

Organization:

Today's Date:

	QUESTION	YOUR ANSWER
1	Do you send targeted emails to prospects based on information from both marketing automation and CRM? (Audience segmentation)	
2	Do you know where your revenue-driving leads come from? (Source ROI reporting)	
3	Is your data clean, free of duplicates, and structured for reporting? (Data preparedness)	
4	Do you use gated content to capture leads on your website? (Gated content marketing)	
5	Do you nurture your buyers in separate, relevant tracks? (Multiple nurture campaigns)	
6	Is your sales team trained and actively using marketing automation inside your CRM? (Sales trained and using)	
7	Do you separately rate your leads for their activity and quality? (Two-dimensional lead rating)	
8	Do you test what messaging drives the most engagement in emails or landing pages? (A/B testing)	
9	Do you automatically change web or email content based on the recipient's segment? (Advanced dynamic content)	
10	Do you know what marketing actions drive the most engagement and revenue? (Multi-touch attribution)	
	TOTAL YOUR SCORE: **CHESHIRE SUCCESS INDEX: MARKETING AUTOMATION**	

SECTION I

THE FOUNDATIONAL PHASE

The first phase is the **Foundational Phase**. This is where you put in the work and get things set up to launch. There are three core elements to focus on here. You're looking at understanding your buyer, setting up reporting and tracking so you have an ROI for your marketing effort, and finally, cleaning up your data. Looking to make sure you've eliminated your duplicates and your data actually sets you up to do the additional reporting that will tell you what actions are driving the most results.

I can't stress enough how important this phase is. If you just did one phase out of all these steps, the Foundational Phase would have the most impact. Everything else stands on this one—hence the name. Every other element of the CSI refers back to this phase.

CHAPTER 3

UNDERSTANDING & SEGMENTING YOUR BUYER

***CSI Question Number One:** Do you send targeted emails to prospects based on information from both marketing automation and CRM?*

Remember that old TV show, *The Newlywed Game*? Imagine four newlywed couples who each think they know their partner very well. The host would ask the husbands or wives a series of questions while their partners are offstage wearing soundproof headphones. After the questions had been asked, the spouse would come back on stage, and the couples would be quizzed to see if they could guess what their significant others answered. Hilarity ensues as couples sometimes hit the right answer but more often than not wildly miss in silly and often embarrassing ways. The craziest questions, and the most partner-elbowing ones, involved questions around things like "making whoopee."

What millions of viewers saw was how even people who have presumably dated, gotten married, and maybe even done the whoopee thing don't really know each other as well as they think. If married couples may not know each other that well, then how much more out of touch are we with our buyers? Like the couples on the screen, we've got our hunches, but there's so much more to learn.

Knowing your buyer is the cornerstone of everything else marketers do.

Knowing your buyer is the cornerstone of everything else marketers do. This is why this chapter comes first. Even though our CSI question "Do you send targeted emails to prospects based on information from both marketing automation and CRM?" seems to focus on the tactic of sending emails, it actually poses a deeper and more important question. Do you know your audience well enough to ensure that you can break it up into targeted groups so that what you're sending is relevant and timely, and therefore more likely to compel their engagement?

In order to be relevant to someone, we need to be able to identify what sets them apart from the crowd. There can be no effective buyer segmentation if you don't actually know your buyers and how to categorize them. The result of this confusion is generic email blasts to entire databases, which guarantees much lower engagement rates despite your hard work.

In this chapter we're going to fix this once and for all, starting with identifying the pitfalls and traps that keep us from really understanding our buyers. We'll then shift to the strategies that high-growth organizations use to truly understand and serve their buyers.

TRAPS TO MISUNDERSTANDING OUR BUYERS

Have you ever seen a TV commercial that you absolutely hated? One of the most entertaining displays of advertising bucks is during the annual Super Bowl, which, according to Lauren Watters of the American Marketing Association, charged $5 million for a thirty-second spot in 2018.[1]

During the broadcast, millions of people around the world turn into advertising critics. There are usually some amazing wins and equally bizarre losses, and almost always you'll hear people complain, "I can't believe they spent five million on *that*."

Marketers have a different perspective and are often even more incredulous about the ads that so obviously fall flat. We know that large investments like Super Bowl advertising don't happen without a lot of meetings and decisions. Yet, despite the marketing and advertising professionals involved in all of those meetings, something was definitely missing, and that's a keen understanding of their target audience.

True, some Super Bowl ads that don't resonate with you weren't intended to if you aren't a typical consumer of that type of product. However, it's also likely that some of the products' teams who came up with the commercial's strategy fell into our first trap: we assume our buyers are just like us. Too often we think we're the buyer, and we design ads and content according to our own values, motivators, and sales goals as opposed to the buyer's needs.

I can assure you that even marketers marketing to marketers

---

1 Andrew Gould, "Super Bowl Ads 2018: Latest Info on Cost of 2018 Super Bowl Commercials," Bleacher Report, February 4, 2018, https://bleacherreport.com/articles/2757119-super-bowl-ads-2018-latest-info-on-cost-of-2018-super-bowl-commercials.

need to be careful not to assume they know everything about their buyers. Acknowledging potential bias goes a long way in reducing it, and it also helps expose the second myth standing in the way of us getting to know our potential: we only need to concern ourselves with one type of buyer.

Perhaps an organization is targeting, for example, C-suite buyers, and ignoring the potential for targeting influencers down the chain. These influencers may not be making the purchase decision, but they could be feeling a pain and urging leadership to make a change, and therefore are a potential buyer to target in your marketing.

Marketers' understandable obsession with metrics can be a blessing and a curse. From the number of clicks to conversions and eventually revenue, one of the strengths of marketing, especially now with marketing automation, is its ability to track almost everything. However, this strength can become the final trap if we're not careful.

Adele Revella, CEO and founder, Buyer Persona Institute, "No Bullsh*t Buyer Personas"

It's easy to get lost in the numbers and graphs and forget that behind each number is an actual person. Take, for instance, a column that shows "130 leads." Assuming our duplicates are under control, that number is actually 130 unique individuals—with their own hopes, dreams, fears, and families!

This concept has been expressed beautifully in the phrase "H2H" that has circulated many marketing circles of late. While I don't encourage dropping the B2B/B2C distinctions, the idea that we are humans marketing to humans is an important one. Whether you're building an email or series of them, remember that actual people are going to decide whether to read what you're sending. Similar to the golden rule, you do not want to market to anyone in a way that you yourself wouldn't appreciate.

Another advantage of an H2H mindset is that it creates a perfect foundation from which you can get to know your buyers. As a number, your buyer is overreduced to simple logic: "Did they click or not?" But a human buyer has feelings! They have a job, a boss, stress, challenges, and worry! The solution your own company offers them should alleviate some of their pain. As a marketer there is a noble purpose to learning what keeps your buyer up at night and guiding them into a solution.

UNDERSTANDING OUR BUYERS

My beautiful wife, Tina, and I love watching shows on Netflix that seek out kindhearted people and surprise them with life-changing gifts. Like ambassadors for the universe, these shows share what happens when selfless people get a much-deserved reward, symbolic of a giant "thank you" from all of us. When I see the tears of appreciation well in the eyes of these unsung heroes, I can't help but get a little choked up myself!

Ardath Albee, CEO and B2B marketing strategist, Marketing Interactions, "Creating Buyer Personas That Drive Content Strategy"

Have you experienced something similar? What is that feeling?

It's empathy. We've all heard that word before, but most of us confuse it with sympathy. We also regularly confuse the two in our marketing, and the results are terrible.

I host my own podcast called *The Hard Corps Marketing Show*, in which I interview fellow marketers, scientists, doctors, salespeople, and others about issues relating to the marketing industry. I was enlightened during a conversation with Kasim Aslam on the podcast, who shared an awesome video created by Brené Brown that graphically presents the difference between sympathy and empathy like this: a person is in a hole. The hole symbolizes the challenge or pain facing a person. Sympathy, defined by Google as "feelings of pity or sorrow for someone else's misfortune," was demonstrated as someone standing on the surface and looking down to the person in the hole. The person looking down says: "Ooo! It looks bad, uh-huh. You want a sandwich?"

Sympathy: Feelings of pity or sorrow for someone else's misfortune.

But empathy, defined as "the ability to understand and share the feelings of another," was demonstrated by the other person climbing down into the hole with the suffering person. Looking around, the climber understood the situation firsthand and simply said, "I know what it's like down here, and you're not alone."

Empathy: The ability to understand and share the feelings of another.

"Empathy fuels connection," Brown explains, "and sympathy drives disconnection. Empathy is a vulnerable choice. In order to connect with you, I have to connect with something inside myself that knows that feeling."

As marketers, how many times have we paid surface-level attention to the challenges of our buyers? Have we created content for content's sake or to actually make a difference? It's a tough challenge, but it's one we need to take stock of and own the results, good or bad.

Most marketers aren't actually trying to trick their buyers. I think it's more that we hope the content is helpful. Clearly that's no longer enough, so it's time to climb in!

A FRAMEWORK FOR CLIMBING IN

We've decided to join our buyers in the hole of their challenges, but we need a way to climb to them. This is best done by one-on-one interviews, compiling the results into **buyer personas**. There is a lot of confusion in the marketing world around personas, so we'll tackle this first and then discuss how to nail those interviews.

"Most of what passes for buyer personas are actually buyer profiles," explained Adele Revella in her conversation with me on the podcast. Revella literally wrote the book on understanding our buyers, *Buyer Personas: How to Gain Insight into Your Customer's Expectations, Align your Marketing Strategies, and Win More Business* (2015). She helped me realize that much of what I thought I knew about buyer personas was misguided, and most of the information we gather about our buyers isn't even actionable.

Like many marketers, my long-held impression of buyer personas was that they included a name like "Marketing Mary," a photo to humanize them, and then some factoids about their generalized collective lives. "Marketing Mary is twenty-eight, has two cats, and loves chocolate." Better personas would then have the typical job responsibilities and the challenges Mary faced in her role.

What I've just described is actually a buyer profile. There's nothing wrong with compiling information on your buyer like this. The value of creating a buyer profile is, first, that you're thinking about and researching the general demographics of your future customers. Anything that drives us to focus our attention on the buyers themselves is a win in my book. While the information isn't as actionable as a buyer persona, it's a good start in the process of customizing your marketing to buyer groups.

So many times, I encounter a busy marketer who emails their entire list the same content. My first recommendation is always a simple question: instead of emailing everyone all at the same time, what about emailing two separate groups? And if you knew you were sending two emails this month, how would you separate your buyers into two larger groups?

Buyer profile research often provides the information you need to do initial segmentation. The straightforward demographics may indicate that your lists should likely be separated by industry or role in a company.

But despite good intentions, most marketers don't build buyer profiles, often because there isn't time and other work takes priority. I would argue that this happens because these profiles don't seem to do anything or drive any action.

Revella said, "I want to make the distinction between profiling a person, who could be your buyer, and understanding their journey, understanding their decision, understanding what you need to do to have them buy from you."

Do you see the difference? The buyer profile isn't all bad. Having a template for what your buyer looks like (i.e., age, financial status, lifestyle, region, responsibilities, challenges, etc.) is a great framework to build on, but it's only the surface of what you're trying to discover about them.

For example, you know your buyer has a dog, certain responsibilities at work, and several challenges. You have to ask yourself, "What does that profile instruct me to do next?" It's not completely devoid of action; you may seek to create content related to the challenges. But the larger question to ask yourself is, "What are we going to do to reduce the friction in the buying experience and encourage action?"

Buyer personas are created within the context of a final goal—in many cases, a purchase of your product or service. "What research did the buyer do? Whom do they trust? What were their steps during the journey? What's going on in their mind? How do they come to these conclusions of whether or not they should do business with us?"

While a profile exists to identify someone's characteristics, a persona records the steps a buyer takes to make a decision, the friction they experienced along the way, and ultimately the reasons they used to buy or not buy. A persona gets inside their mindset so we can encourage them and customize our marketing to create the buyer's journey they need. Information for buyer profiles can be gathered via traditional marketing activities like forms and surveys, but personas require deeper conversations.

Ellen Naylor, CEO, Business Intelligence Source, "Win/Loss for the Win"

A typical buyer profile might suggest your customer is in their forties, is an IT manager, has a college degree, and enjoys Comic-Con. It might also suggest that they're friendly based on the random photo chosen from LinkedIn. Many are given names too. This IT manager is "Bob," and so you refer to him in conversations.

What I've described is the surface level of getting to know your buyer. Most companies don't do profiles. There just isn't time for a nice-to-have project like this. Intrinsically, we can perceive the lack of direction from these documents. The same questions still linger: "How does Bob research solutions? What is Bob's preferred way to engage with sales? What about our product or service is most valuable to Bob and why?"

Digging below the surface of a profile, we find buried treasure! Bob can keep his name and picture, but with a buyer persona we can now answer those questions. Bob trusts analyst reports and thinks review sites are rigged. He often researches future tech on the weekends because he enjoys staying current. Being informed is important for his job security too. When it comes to dealing with sales, Bob prefers calls that have a sales engineer so he can get his advanced questions answered. He's also going to need to sell this new purchase to three different people in his organization … the list goes on!

Tell me what you could do differently when marketing to Bob. Oh, and on that note: that buyer profile whom we call Bob? It turns out that two distinct personas were hiding inside that one profile. Bob A and Bob B buy in completely different ways.

A large global manufacturer once contracted with Revella to do buyer interviews and build out buyer personas for a specific division. The company serviced multiple geographies, languages, industries, and buyers. How many personas, or separate buying experiences, do you think they had when the interviews were complete?

Only two.

That's right. There were two distinct buyer journeys at the end of the day across all of the different demographics. Simplifying a bit, one persona wanted to see success stories and to speak with a knowledgeable sales rep right away. The other definitely didn't want to speak to anyone, preferring instead to see a comparison chart on how the product stacked up to the other models.

Understanding these differences allowed the manufacturer to serve their personas with exactly what they were looking for. Two distinct marketing paths were created with content to support them. The additional demographic factors such as geographies, industries, and role were addressed with dynamic content.

You can see how in this example, a company without personas would naturally pursue a segmentation strategy that tries to cover every geography, every industry, and any other factor. That's a lot of additional work! In the face of so many to-dos, many marketers toss up the white flag and only create a single generic segment.

In order to understand your buyer's journey and build a true persona, you need to spend time talking with customers and prospects.

However, by better understanding the factors that are important to our buyers and grouping similar paths together into a persona, we not only serve our buyers better but become more efficient marketers!

As you can probably imagine, in order to understand your buyer's journey and build a true persona, you need to spend time talking with customers and prospects.

THE BUYER INTERVIEW

Marketers rarely create opportunities to have conversations with current customers or potential buyers. As with many of technology's advances—from social media to surveys—the intention to make us more connected often results in the opposite. Empowered with empathy and the persona framework, we need to have deeper discussions to really understand the buyer's journey.

Buyer personas are created by interviewing your customers. That's where the magic happens. It's a specific kind of interview, and this is the scary part for a lot of people. But the reason we don't often know as much about our buyers as we should comes down to poor interviewing tactics. And a lot of the challenge around interviewing comes from the various obstacles of getting in front of a real customer, as well as knowing what questions to ask once we do.

Your mission is to find someone who, in the last year, has been involved in the buying decision. Keep in mind that these people aren't just your customers. The ones who didn't select you are equally helpful too. Recent buyers are important because, over time, you forget details, and it can take more skill to extract insights from those you've been involved with beyond a year. Ideally, you don't want anyone from your company who was involved in the sales process asking the questions. That personal bias can get in the way. Start with ten customers who chose your product and ten who decided not to purchase.

A great opening question I learned from Revella is this: "Take me back to the day when you first decided to evaluate ________ (e.g., a solution, service, product) and tell me what happened."

That's it! It gets your buyer talking! And talking. And talking ...

How do I know? Because Revella interviewed me live on my podcast about my journey when I first purchased marketing automation. If you'd like to hear an example of a master at work, check out the episode. In the interview, you'll see that she asks plenty of follow-up questions, and the insights she gained on my buying experience came from that very personal, one-on-one dialogue.

The follow-up question is the real power of the buyer interview and something surveys simply can't duplicate. It involves picking up on the context, tone of voice, and subject of the initial response. Ask "why" to the initial responses to really understand what is being said.

What worked or didn't work in each of those cases? Are there any recurring themes?

Equipped with questions and an inquisitive mindset, get out there and start having conversations with your buyers to learn about who they are and what they really want. Do it the old-fashioned way and actually talk to them, getting to know who they really are. The insights will help you form buyer personas that will transform the way you market and sell!

THE PATH OF SEGMENTATION

The more conversations you have with your buyers, the easier it will be to segment them for marketing. Emailing everyone all at once creates a terrible experience for a buyer, but creating ten versions of each email creates a terrible experience for the marketer! There isn't a happy middle but rather a progression of segmentation strategies as you build or rebuild your marketing automation program.

Start with a "Catchall" Segment

This initial step isn't really a segment but a starting point. For many organizations this is status quo, and many don't need to take action to even get here. At the start of your path to segmentation, it's important that you create valuable content and offer it to all of your buyers.

Parmelee Eastman, President, EastSight Consulting, "Future-Proof Your Marketing"

While it won't be targeted, it's still generally helpful to your average buyer. This step is here so that nurturing can begin today and we don't wait for perfection to take action. These engagements will also help us identify qualifying characteristics about our buyers in the forms they complete to get the initial content we're offering. We'll revisit and perfect nurturing in CSI number six later in this book.

Developing Simple Segmentation

At first, we emailed everyone all at once. In **simple segmentation**, we're looking to divide our whole audience into two or three groups. This will enable us to customize the messages we send, increasing their benefit to our buyers and thus increasing their engagement with our campaigns.

Even though you may serve multiple geographies, industries, and departments, this step is focused on our top two or three buyer groups. Focusing on these groups in the short term will quickly deliver the most results. The remaining groups will continue to be served by the catchall segmentation until we can better address them.

Who should comprise the top segments? How should we identify them? The goal for simple segmentation is to be able to separate buyer groups into a few smaller groups that share common characteristics and have enough potential to make creating marketing specific to them worth it.

The two best examples of simple segments are grouping by industry or the buyer's role in their organization. We can then adjust our tone, terminology, and message to what each segment will find most valuable. If your organization has two or three obvious large groups of buyers that aren't industry or role based, that's okay. You can segment based on other factors as well, such as an account-based marketing approach or product interest. Just remember to keep it simple and focus your efforts on a few main segments.

BUYER PERSONA–BASED SEGMENTATION

This type of segmentation is the final and most effective. I encourage you to begin interviewing buyers as soon as you can. It will take time to plan, contact, schedule, and interview them. It's for this practical reason that simple segmentation came first. When your research zeroes in on one or two buyer personas, though, it will be a relief! While you may have addressed several simple segments and had planned on expanding many more, most marketers find that they have far fewer personas. The benefit of this is that not only will you create an awesome experience for your buyers, but you won't need to create assets for all of those industries you wanted to address.

Whether you're using profiles or personas, once you have your segmentation model figured out, you need only to input the criteria into your marketing automation platform's lists and watch them stay up to date. Pardot has dynamic lists that will constantly check to see who in your database fits certain criteria and add them to the segmentation. Rather magically, those who no longer fit the criteria are automatically removed from the lists.

Those dynamic lists can activate who gets specific nurturing campaigns. They can even power dynamic content changes on both your website and in each email. These superpowers will be covered in the upcoming chapters. The work you do now in segmentation will continue to be utilized on almost every future step you take. With that said, don't skip the work in this section!

We can take Adele's advice in our everyday marketing strategy by going deep in our curiosity about our customers and empowering our automation to keep lists up to date. Acknowledge the surface-level details, and then inquire beyond them to find what really goes into that buying decision.

CHAPTER 4

SOURCE ROI

CSI Question Number Two: Do you know where your revenue-driving leads come from?

Are trade shows and events a part of your marketing efforts? For one of our clients, they were the primary lead source, and they participated in over eighty trade shows a year. Each event required significant expenses, including a booth shipped to the location and staff flown in to work the show floors. While good leads were being generated from these efforts, they had no idea which shows were actually responsible for sales. Something was working, but without proper ROI tracking, they became hostage to the events! They had to keep doing all of them in fear that if they dropped the wrong shows, they would lose the new business that had historically been generated.

One of the first projects we undertook with these jet-lagged conference goers was to help them set up first-touch ROI tracking in their marketing automation system. Given that the technical part is rather straightforward, most of the work went toward ensuring every lead had an accurate source tagged, and putting proper controls in place to ensure future leads would as well.

As they continued to execute the events and track the efforts, the results started to populate, and they were mind blowing! Roughly thirty of the events were showing positive return after considerable time. This meant they had been spending serious marketing dollars on fifty events with no return. Ouch! The good news is they utilized the ROI data to begin focusing efforts on the successful events, often upgrading their investments. They were also left with a huge budget surplus that they were able to reinvest into other marketing channels.

The number one question in marketing is, "What's working?" and perhaps just as importantly, "What's not working?" If you can answer those questions, you can focus your resources on getting a much higher rate of return on your strategy.

This dramatic story perfectly highlights the importance and power of the second CSI element: Do you know where your revenue-driving leads come from?

In the above example, you can replace the "events" source with any other marketing campaign, and the lesson remains the same. The number one question in marketing is, "What's working?" and perhaps just as importantly, "What's not working?" If you can answer those questions, you can focus your resources on getting a much higher rate of return on your strategy. Aside from better understanding your customers, nothing is more important in marketing.

In this chapter, we'll share stories of first-touch ROI in action and talk through the strategies necessary for getting actionable insights. We'll also briefly talk about the fickle challenge of multitouch attribution while saving the good parts for CSI number ten: advanced reporting and attribution.

Michael Brenner, CEO, Marketing Insider Group, "The Quest for Content Marketing ROI"

First Things First

Understanding what's working and what's not in your own strategy starts with the first touch. Through digital tracking, the number one thing we're trying to accomplish is aligning marketing with revenue. First-touch source reporting, or source ROI reporting, is the practical, achievable first step in aligning everything you do in marketing toward generating revenue for your company.

Because of that, "Do you know where your revenue-driving leads come from?" is the second question on our CSI questionnaire. This step is near the top of the CSI maturity model because first-touch ROI reporting should be your first key reporting metric as you work toward a revenue-focused marketing strategy.

Why?

First of all, it's easy. Say what? Yes, it's easy. In most marketing automation platform solutions, it's literally out-of-the-box functionality that's readily configurable. You just have to set it up and use it. Oftentimes that simply involves tagging your sources, and you're off to the first-touch-tracking races.

Second, it's quick. Most marketing automation platforms provide users with the ability to update sources rather easily, so if you haven't tagged them before and you still have the data, you can enrich your sources by uploading the information. And if any of those sources were tied to revenue, most programs will reflect it instantly. Any newly gained leads might take a little more time to bake, but you'll know you're fully tracking.

Last, it's definitive! After configuring your platform for first-touch ROI reporting, you'll see your lead sources listed out with the number of leads each one generated, as well as the number that progressed through the marketing funnel stages you've established. And knowing how many closed deals came from which specific sources is incredibly helpful when tweaking campaigns to yield an even stronger ROI.

ROI

Marketing automation technology acts as both a web-capture platform and an emailing hub, while also tying directly into sales opportunities and tracking in your CRM. And from that, the sales you generate are directly correlated to the original activity that first acquired the lead. But be leery here; there are a couple of traps!

The first culprit is mistakenly replacing ROI with activity tracking. Tracking the marketing activity you do is no replacement for understanding the business results from a marketing investment. While individually they both have merit, mixing them up creates unreadable reports.

The second trap is going too detailed too fast. I've seen a lot of manual work spent tracking the tiniest of buyer actions. Marketing automation systems can track clicks and opens easily. Those numbers are helpful with tactical execution but pale in comparison to the final question: Did they end up purchasing our product or service?

You see it's more important to know the location you found someone than the thing that interested them. Their interest and reason for engaging is good data you can utilize, but first things first! If I know the location in the pond where the fish are biting, I need to navigate my fishing boat to that location before I start fiddling with what lure attracted the fish. And your best lure won't catch any fish on land!

Jim Lenskold, President, Lenskold Group, Inc., "Ripping Open Marketing ROI"

I had a chance to speak with Jim Lenskold on my podcast. Jim is a global expert on revenue planning and marketing ROI who wrote the book *Marketing ROI: How to Plan, Measure, and Optimize Strategies for Profit*. Jim is an awesome guy and a serious thought leader in the industry, and I learned so much from him through his book and our conversation.

Jim's advice is to fill out a plan ahead of time before investing in a campaign or a particular source to get leads. The plan doesn't have to be extravagant, but it should define how much the investment is anticipated to cost, how many leads you expect to get from that investment, and how many of those leads will make it through the buyer's journey funnel and result in a sale. We know not every lead will convert, but if we're strategic about it, we can forecast with relative accuracy how many of those sources will move through that funnel.

TYPES OF SOURCES

When you identify your first touch incorrectly, the results range from general confusion to outright insanity by continuing to invest money in channels that don't deliver.

Many marketers I meet at user groups and after presentations share their confusion about campaigns and first-touch sources with me. To make matters worse, many consultants and technology providers themselves muddle the waters!

> When you identify your first touch incorrectly, the results range from general confusion to outright insanity by continuing to invest money in channels that don't deliver.

Imagine that you were able to convince your leadership that a test of Google Search ads was a good idea for your organization. You want to spend $5,000 and then evaluate. It's a smart channel to test. Leads coming from Google typically convert well because they're actively searching for a solution.

After creating the ads and testing them for several weeks, you look at the results. Without first-touch ROI tracking set up, you'll be relying on subjective commentary of those involved. If a sales rep has a couple of bad calls with a few of the leads in the pool, he might write off the whole campaign and convince his managers that it's a terrible source of leads. What if it actually is a fantastic source of leads? Or isn't? Without source information, it's like rolling dice with a really important decision.

THE HARD CORPS MARKETING SHOW
EPISODE #093

Peter Fader, Professor of marketing, Wharton Business School, "The Customer Abundance Formula"

So what are sources? First, let's talk about what sources are *not*.

Your website isn't a source. Some systems will call it a source, but it's not. People don't just dream up your web address. And while your website can be a good catchall sometimes, it just means the first thing we've tracked customers to was your website. However, the goal is to increase both your tagging and source tracking so the website category is reduced as low as possible. By itself it's not a great goal, as it doesn't necessarily tell you what you can take action on and where to go to get more leads.

Email isn't a source either. People don't just receive your email address from the sky and then go to your website. They were on a list that you acquired, or they were forwarded to you by a friend.

Webinars also aren't technically lead sources. People didn't just magically hear about your webinar and decide to attend. That's the marketing action that they participated in and the offer that they were willing to sign up for. Putting this concept into a real-world example, I present at least two webinars a month, and each one focuses on a specific element of the CSI. We promote these webinars across all of our social channels. Let's say you saw a post about my ROI webinar on LinkedIn, clicked on the link, and then registered on the landing page. What is your first touch? Many marketers incorrectly answer "webinars." The webinar was the trigger that elicited your interest, but where did you first learn about the webinar? It was on LinkedIn! So the source of you as a lead might be listed as "Social—LinkedIn—Organic." We've added "Organic" because you found a socially shared post, not a LinkedIn ad.

A source is the channel that brought you in and not the reason you signed up. It's the reason a lead found out about an engagement activity like a webinar. Did the lead discover the webinar from a sales rep? Perhaps from an AdWords campaign that linked to the registration page? Did they learn about it from a partner's event? Those are all sources.

The key is to make sure you identify the lead source accurately whenever you can, but as you'll see, there are sources of traffic that can be difficult to track.

DARK TRAFFIC

Dark traffic comprises the visitors to your site that have come via a way you can't track or may have mislabeled. Typically, websites will have at least 20 percent or more of this mysterious inbound traffic, and when your sources are not properly tagged, these rates can quickly climb.

David Meiselman, CMO, ezCater, "My Marketing Mentor Talks Measurement"

Imagine you invested a portion of your marketing budget into creating a brand podcast with its own microsite. It begins to take hold, and the word gets out that it's the source of truth in your industry. Many of the subscribers from the show click from the microsite onto your main site. Without Pardot tracking code on the microsite or tracked links, you receive a bunch of traffic from this effort and don't know which marketing program gets the credit. It could be driving a consistent number of leads, but without that information, you might be tempted to shut down the effort and redirect the budget elsewhere. Dark traffic strikes again.

There are a couple of ways to combat the dark traffic problem, so let's explore that briefly.

The first is through putting campaign-specific marketing automation tracking on code on all of the websites you control. When you create a campaign in your marketing automation platform, it automatically generates a unique tracking code. Pasting this tracking code in the source code of the web page for that particular campaign allows visitors and prospects to automatically be associated or tagged with that campaign. A great example of taking tagging to another level is using separate tracking code for your main website, your blog, and any microsites you have. This will help alleviate the dark traffic because you'll be able to isolate the performance of your SEO and blogging efforts as well as any branded efforts like the podcast example above.

Another way to minimize dark traffic is to plan for all the sources you will have, keep an active tally of them, and ensure you're using campaign-specific parameters in each inbound link. Most marketing automation systems can pick up on the sources that are indicated in the link. I always recommend that marketers create a spreadsheet with all known sources. In addition to keeping things organized, you can write formulas to automatically append campaign parameters to links.

In the process of attacking dark traffic, avoid asking your customers for their lead source. In the past, online forms or even offline paperwork used to ask, "Where did you hear about us?" Not only is this a bad customer experience, but every field on a form decreases the number of people who complete it. This says nothing to the fact that many people incorrectly fill it out!

Also, don't ask sales to manually track lead sources either. Historically, such requests are fraught with challenges and produce inaccurate data. Usually it's a case of a sales rep not caring about this data field and skipping it, or worse, just making something up. Improperly incentivized sales reps could also select themselves as the lead source after making the call and realizing it's a qualified deal. Whether done intentionally or not, it happens. And when marketing and sales alignment is in a state of open warfare, grabbing credit for leads is common, as you've probably seen before. Good luck optimizing your campaign when that's going on!

The best solution is to use lead source tagging in your marketing automation technology platform to illuminate the dark traffic without introducing human error into the process. When you nail the source ROI tracking step in the Foundational Phase, you'll be able to confidently seek out new leads from a variety of sources knowing your marketing automation strategy is on the right path.

CHAPTER 5

DATA PREPAREDNESS

CSI Question Number Three: Is your data clean, free of duplicates, and structured for reporting?

In a close football game between the Philadelphia Eagles and Chicago Bears in 2019, Cody Parkey successfully kicked a field goal, only to have to repeat it minutes later. The opposing coach, Doug Pederson, had called a time-out right before the successful kick. They call this "icing the kicker." It gives him several minutes to consider if he can kick it again, and unfortunately for Parkey, the tactic worked, and he missed his second try.

Misses like this are great metaphors for the misses that happen in our data. We never *intend* to miss the kick, get our data wrong, upset our customers, and flop a deal with bad data, but it happens. And while we don't exactly have a team actively trying to get us to screw up, the data itself is often our opposing team, as it continually needs care.

Data can be your best friend, but untended it can convince you that walking off a cliff is a good idea.

> Data can be your best friend, but untended it can convince you that walking off a cliff is a good idea.

With data, we have a marvelous contrast of challenge and reward. An Dun & Bradstreet study showed that less than half of B2B companies trust their data.[2] Meanwhile, a Campaign Monitor study highlights that companies that properly segment their lists have seen average increases in revenue of 760 percent![3]

DATA CHALLENGES

Bad data hurts. It costs US businesses more than $611 billion each year and hurts in many different ways.[4] The first is the damage it does to sales by hurting the sales situation both in the now and in the future.

In the now, bad data hurts the relationship with your consumer. It makes for ineffective campaigns, which give way to disengaged buyers. If the engagement of the buyer is suffering, then they're not learning about your product or service. And if they aren't learning about your product or service, then they likely aren't buying either.

---

2 "The B2B Activation Priority: Mature Firms Reap Benefits of Data Activation," A Forrester Consulting Thought Leadership Paper Commissioned By Dun & Bradstreet, May 2018, https://www.dnb.com/content/dam/english/economic-and-industry-insight/forrester-b2b-data-activation-priority-2018.pdf.

3 "The New Rules of Email Marketing," Campaign Monitor, accessed November 2, 2019, https://www.campaignmonitor.com/resources/guides/email-marketing-new-rules/.

4 Cornelia Cozmiuc, "Poor Marketing Data Costs Online Businesses $611 Billion Per Year," CognitiveSEO, accessed November 2, 2019, https://cognitiveseo.com/blog/13094/poor-marketing-data/.

You're not only hurting the current campaign, but the future sales are getting stung as well. With bad data in play, not only is a prospect less likely to purchase, but you're also likely to earn a poor reputation. Stories of your poor segmentation and other data challenges will make for good networking story fodder at the next B2B meetup. You don't want your company to be associated with poor marketing.

Karen Steele, CCO, LeanData Inc., "Revenue-Centric Marketing"

Not only does your reputation as a company take a hit at marketing events, but your email reputation takes a hit with email servers as well. When you're sending emails with bad data—such as emails with the wrong salutation, name, or topic—it just looks bad. You get far more spam complaints and unsubscribes from people when they have been treated the wrong way with bad data. When you get more spam complaints, that message goes out to all the servers, and your deliverability rates will plummet. When that happens, customers with even good data may not be getting your message.

Second of all, it actually gets worse over time. I remember getting to a company and inheriting a CRM and marketing tool that had thirty thousand records in it. Unfortunately, only a couple of thousand were recent. Most of them would span back several decades. Unfortunately, the majority of these records were useless by this point because most people had moved jobs, retired, or even passed away. Even worse, if I used that information, I'd get dinged for sending bad emails by the servers because you look like a spammer with inaccurate data. That's because either people tagged the emails as spam or the message was sent to an email address that didn't exist. Any time your server starts seeing a lot of emails being returned to sender, that's a surefire way to get yourself marked as a spam account.

Joe Andrews, VP of product and solution marketing at InsideView, came onto the podcast recently with some scary information. Joe estimates that 5.3 million Americans changed jobs last month. That means your data is decaying, and it's getting worse over time. The longer it sits around, the more likely it is to get dirty. It's simply not going to stay clean for very long any more. It becomes more inaccurate every day. You have to have ways of keeping your data accurate and up to date.

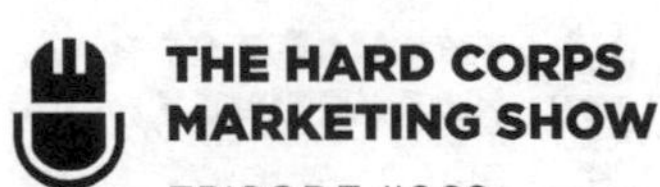

Joe Andrews, VP of product and solution marketing, InsideView, "Marketing with Data Confidence"

There's a multiplying cost of dirty data, as well. The longer you wait to clean your data, the harder and more expensive it becomes to deal with. Data scientists actually refer to this as the 1-10-100 rule. The idea is that it takes a dollar to confirm the accuracy of a record while it's being entered, because it just takes a moment. But it takes $10 to clean it and de-duplicate it if you're waiting until later. If nothing is done, $100 is the cost due to lost opportunities and wasted resources. Arguably, a lost opportunity costs way more than $100. That's more like a lost lead at $100. A lost opportunity could be tens of thousands to millions of dollars, depending on what your company sells.

DATA PRIORITIES

Preparing marketing data ties into two key areas. The first is **creating email lists** and segmentation, which comes from all the work we did when learning about our buyer personas. We need to be able to access and understand who fits where and who should get what email. We want to make sure our lists are clean and strong and full of data that we can actually use. Additionally, we want to be prepared for email by creating those lists and then dropping in information. We want to make sure that we don't have too many duplicates, that we're sending messages to the right addresses, and that we have permission to send to them.

Second, we want to be prepared for **reporting**. There's a common phrase: "Trash in, trash out." The quality of your data is often dependent on the quality of your reporting. If you have bad data going in, then you're often going to have bad data in your reports. That could be bad because you may make decisions for your company, and your marketing, based on the results of the report. Best case, the report doesn't tell you anything. Worst case, you make strategic decisions based on incorrect data. So let's read the CSI challenge together: Is your data clean, free of duplicates, and structured for reporting?

FIXING YOUR DATA

Now that we know the goal, let's talk about how you get there. For the record, almost every marketing data expert has their own words for the following steps, processes, and strategies. I've used ones that resonate most with me, but just keep in mind that the terminology is not as important as the strategies themselves. Furthermore, there are great data vendors out there, and often their services combine several big steps. The order in which you take these steps is important. Make sure not to skip any; otherwise you might find yourself back in the exact same situation a year later.

First you want to **assess**. You'll never find me shying away from pausing the action to take in the current situation and plan next steps. You, too, need to pause and assess the current level of poor data, duplicates, and gaps in your reporting. Doing so will ensure that you can actually use the data at the end of this process. You're looking for inaccurate data, missing data, and duplicates, as well as misnamed data. Put simply, how is the data labeled? Do you have a different field? Do you call someone something different in your field than sales does in theirs? If so, it might be the same bits of data just named differently.

Next, you'll want to **clean your data**. It's messy in there, and after assessing it, you have a good understanding of what's going on. In addition to the gaps you've identified, here are several key areas to address. First, email. Ensure that you have valid email addresses. Use this opportunity to get rid of all duplicates. A good marketing automation system will prevent duplicates based on unique factors, like email. Pardot does this automatically, unless you turn it off. Note to self: Don't turn it off.

After you clean your data, you need to verify your system's **field integrity**. Fields should contain one piece of data per field. That means you should even divide first and last names into separate fields. Why? Because you'll want the first name for email greetings and for personalization. Drop-down menus are best. Whenever you can use drop-down menus on forms, it helps ensure that the data going in is something you can control. Use them whenever and wherever you can. This comes up a lot with the title field. I avoid asking for people's titles like a plague and choose instead to ask for their role. I get the real answer I wanted anyways, without the ambiguity that comes from people with crazy titles, like "chief awesome officer."

Then set up your **standards and formatting** system. For

instance, is it "New York" spelled out, "NY," or "NYC"?" Decide and standardize all informational inputs across both marketing automation and CRM systems.

David Raab, Marketing data consultant and founder, CDP Institute, "Marketing Data with CDP Institute"

Next, get rid of **unsubscribers**. If they haven't engaged or been sent to sales, delete them. They're taking up space in the system that you're likely paying for. The good news with a system like Pardot is that prospects are never totally deleted. If the prospect comes back, their record gets revived and all the data that came with it. Best of both worlds.

Finally, **protect your data**. It's critically important to set up systems and processes to protect the existing data, and to watch over your changes to the system. What's the point of cleaning all this data if by tomorrow it's dirty again?

There are two main focus areas when it comes to protecting your data. The first is new data entering the system, and the other is managing how data gets changed once it's in the system. Before you begin investigating either area, make sure you're looking at the entire customer journey and all of the departments that have access to your systems. Setting up protocols to ensure marketing is changing data properly is only part of the story if sales, customer service, and accounting all have access too.

Let's begin with new data entering the system. How do new leads, contacts, and general data come into the system? Typically, every organization has marketing automation–generated leads that complete forms. People fill out forms, and then their information is captured and fed from the marketing system into the CRM at the appropriate time.

Another source comes from the marketing department manually uploading lists. Oftentimes these lists come from events, such as conferences or expos, that the team has attended. Commonly, when you're scanning badges, you generate huge lists of leads to add into your system, as well as third-party vendors that come from purchases and other campaigns you've run outside of your system.

Sales needs the ability to add new leads or contacts based on their reach out to the existing leads. People often pass the buck on follow-up calls.

Keep in mind that sales is more than likely generating leads on their own. At the very minimum, sales needs the ability to add new leads or contacts based on their reach out to the existing leads. People often pass the buck on follow-up calls. "Oh, no. I'm not the right person for that call. You should call my coworker, who is the decision maker in this situation. Here's their name and number." Now you have a totally new lead. That lead needs to get into the system. Once you have a good understanding of where the leads come from, put the controls in place to ensure data coming in follows all the rules you established when cleaning up your data. What fields are required for a lead? What format does the data need to be in? Essentially, ensure there is a process in place to only bring in the data that would pass all of the clean checks. Remember, data decays at an alarming rate, so be really careful about bringing in any older data.

Next, you need to turn your attention to understanding how the data gets changed. When second and third forms are filled out in a marketing automation system, sometimes prospects update or change their information. Those changes may then alter what is in the CRM. Furthermore, marketing might be updating information in the CRM, and certainly sales is making the information more accurate based on their phone calls and emails with the prospects. This presents a classic challenge to avoid, which is the dilemma of having sales and marketing arguing about where a lead came from. Oftentimes a lead might come in and sales may change the lead source in order to reflect the sales-generated lead, whereas maybe marketing created it. Either way, whenever possible, deleting should be turned off, as well as changing important fields like the lead source once the value is set.

ENRICHING YOUR DATA

You can bring in third-party data to supplement what you already have for the purpose of filling in any information gaps and creating more relevant marketing. It's important to keep this goal in mind because there's a lot of useless data out there that has absolutely no bearing on what you need. The quantity of information about your prospects is not nearly as powerful as knowing the single biggest challenge your prospects are facing right now. So what do you want to know? Is there a piece of data that helps you better classify your prospect into appropriate segments or personas? Is there a piece of information that sales needs to know, or that would help them connect with leads?

Grayson Daniels, Director of professional services, Cheshire Impact, "The Magic of Marketing Data"

Two of the most common data enrichment efforts are demographic and geographic, but that may not be the case for your particular product or service. In any case, there are two types of data enrichment methods: **internal** and **external**. Once you've identified data that would be strategic and actionable about your buyer, it's time to figure out how you're going to acquire the desired information. Look to internal data-gathering methods first. Is there something you can ask on a marketing form to get the data? Marketing automation allows us to ask multiple questions every time a prospect completes a form. Additionally, the first person to contact a lead, often a sales development rep (SDR), can qualify a prospect by asking critical questions. Regardless, some people may not want to, or be able to, answer all of the questions. In that case, the data may be best gained through third-party vendors, a.k.a. the external method. Company size is a great example of the need for external data. Most employees aren't aware of the size of their company, even the public ones. Rather than having your prospect guess at the answer, you can use third-party data to quickly assess the size of the account.

Many organizations use third parties to check that their data is accurate as well. Not everyone completes it accurately, even when they're trying to, so having data accuracy supplementation can really pay off in keeping your data clean. Account enrichment is another reason for external data gathering. Like in the company size example above, account data is often vital for B2B sales. If your organization is utilizing a form of account-based marketing, then you'll want to be creating processes to enrich your account data and merge leads in the same organization under the same account for CRM.

Finally, a sound data enrichment program is helpful if you are considering the use of **advanced reporting**. If you plan on reporting campaign effectiveness, as well as multitouch reporting, you need to start tracking those touches sooner rather than later. Having a lot of data, especially data that's most important to your prospect, is the best way to strengthen your reporting capabilities.

With the existing data clean, protected, and enriched with details, it's now time to grow. Next up, the Growth Phase, where marketing shines!

SECTION II

THE GROWTH PHASE

Congratulations! We're in a new phase. This is the **Growth Phase**. With the foundation of your marketing strategy as solid as ever, we can now really crank up our marketing efforts. You'll find **capture** and **nurture** in this phase, two of the four key values of marketing automation. It's a big deal. While only two elements are in this phase, it's very much the bulk of the tactical work you'll do in marketing automation.

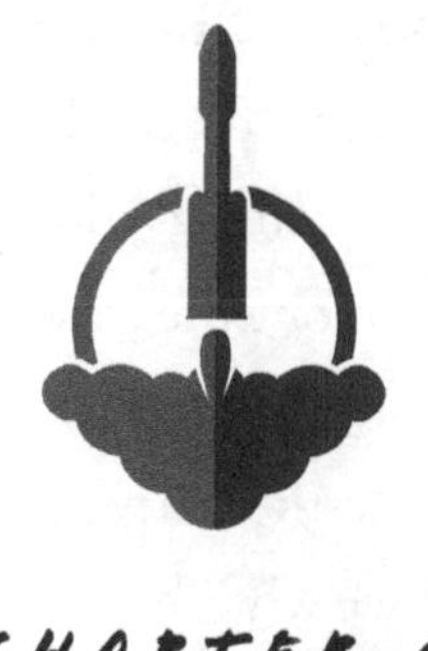

CHAPTER 6

GATED CONTENT MARKETING

CSI Question Number Four: Do you use gated content to capture leads on your website?

A few years ago, I was working with a marketing team from a large financial services organization to improve their overall marketing automation strategy. One of the first things reviewed was their marketing content. I learned they had hired an attorney in New York City at a rate of $1,000 per hour to write a twenty-seven-page white paper. A thousand dollars an hour? I recall wondering if I was in the wrong business!

Intrigued, I asked the team what kind of questions this piece of content answered and how it helped their buyer. All the heads around the table began to slowly sink. No one said anything, and everyone diverted their eyes from mine.

Finally, someone spoke up. "It doesn't," she said. Come to find out, they hadn't approached this piece of content with their buyer in mind. The piece they had created was more of a brag piece, a slick bit of prose that bragged more about the product and the company than addressing the challenges and concerns of potential buyers. They had mentioned wanting to grow the importance of marketing at their company, but now I could see why they were still viewed as the "print shop for sales" internally.

Thankfully, they were eventually able to chop up the content into smaller pieces and highlight parts that were helpful to the buyer. Not a complete loss, but it was a really expensive lesson for them to learn!

> We want to help them in their job, with the work that they do on a regular basis. If we do that, we're going to make some really juicy content that's irresistible to people.

When we create content, we want to do it with the buyer in mind. We want to answer the questions they're going to be asking. We want to help them in their job, with the work that they do on a regular basis. If we do that, we're going to make some really juicy content that's irresistible to people. We're going to get more and more leads out of it, and we're going to help people out at the same time.

HOW MUCH CONTENT DO I NEED?

Oftentimes, when people are looking at buying marketing automation or really cranking up their use of it, they say, "I don't have enough content." Their heart is in the right place, because content is the ammunition for marketing automation. You want to offer value in your emails, on your website, or wherever else, and that means you need good content and plenty of it. It is important, but you don't have to have a million pieces of content to be effective.

My first foray into using marketing automation presented this content challenge to me. Of the seven pieces of content I inherited, only three of them were immediately usable. The first was an interactive online demo, the second piece of content was a case study, and the third piece was a white paper. I ended up creating a series of automations that resembled an upside-down triangle. If a prospect registered to explore the online demo, they were automatically offered the case study the following day. If a different prospect registered for the case study first, they were offered the interactive demo the following day. Anyone who did both was automatically offered the white paper and immediately sent to sales.

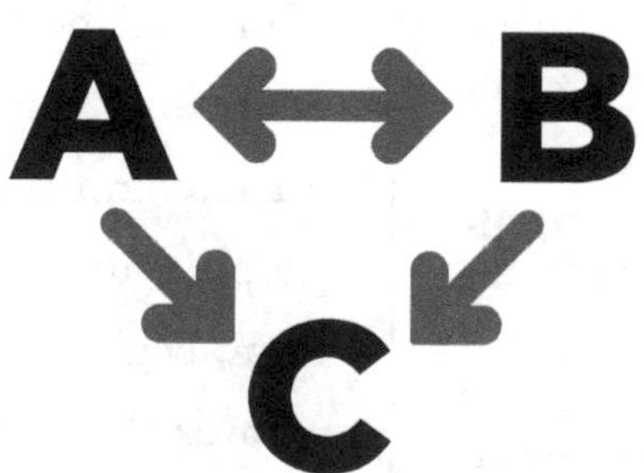

The style of the emails was important too. Rather than coming from marketing, the sales rep, or a fictional person, the emails came from our "solution architect" and industry thought leader. Now, it wasn't actually from him. It was from our marketing automation platform, but it was a personal-looking email with a link to a case study. For example, one of the emails suggested that those who enjoyed the interactive demo found that this case study really helped them understand how the methodology would benefit them in the real world.

Thanks to this approach, a large percentage of buyers who consumed one piece of content went on to engage with the second. Many even replied to the solution architect to thank him for the suggestion! Additionally, those who got on the phone with sales actually knew what was going on. Previously they would ask, "Who are you? What do you do?" But now they were further along in the buying process and often started out by asking for pricing!

Three solid pieces of content were all it took to get the ball rolling. It's not a magic number, just a starting point. After creating that basic setup, I went on to build out more tailored content specific to different buyer personas and industries.

CONTENT MARKETING 101

First, let me just say that whole books can be written on content marketing, and they have been! I'll recommend some amazing people to continue learning from, beginning with some of the wizards that I've talked to on the podcast like Andy Crestodina . But how do you compress volumes into half a chapter?

Robert Rose, Founder and chief troublemaker, The Content Advisory, "The Content Marketing Troublemaker"

We have to go back to our *strategy-process-technology* framework. What we're really focused on here is why it's important and what strategies you need to pursue in order to be successful. How you write the actual piece of content or how you optimize it for SEO, we can leave to other resources.

A great source for all things content is the Content Marketing Institute (CMI). Since 2007, this organization has been a bastion of knowledge. Their goal is to teach, which makes them a solid source without strings attached. The CMI defines content marketing as "a strategic marketing approach focused on creating and distributing valuable, relevant, and consistent content to attract and retain a clearly defined audience—and, ultimately, to drive profitable customer action."[5]

Content marketing: A strategic marketing approach focused on creating and distributing valuable, relevant, and consistent content to attract and retain a clearly defined audience—and, ultimately, to drive profitable customer action.

When it comes to planning out this distribution of value, there are two important documents you need to create. First is your current content index. I'm sure you know the quote, "A bird in the hand is worth two in the bush." Well, one solid piece of content in action is worth ten in the air. Like I said before, you really don't need as much content as you may think, as long as you have a strategic plan on how you will use it. Once you know what you have, you'll go into the next stage of the planning phase: the Buyer Question Map.

STAGE	QUESTIONS ASKED	ANSWER TO QUESTION	BEST MEDIUM TO CONVEY ANSWER
EARLY	How do I get ROI on my marketing?	You set up first touch tracking in Pardot.	One-pager with screenshare video.

5 "What Is Content Marketing?" Content Marketing Institute, accessed November 2, 2019, https://contentmarketinginstitute.com/what-is-content-marketing/.

The Buyer Question Map is your guide to knowing what to write *next*. When completed, you will have an action list for the content you'll need to develop and in prioritized order.

The Buyer Question Map has three columns. The first is the "Questions Asked" column. These are the questions your buyers ask in their daily jobs as well as questions about your product and service. They're going to be listed in order of the stage, and we typically break these stages up into early-, mid-, and late-stage questions. You can be more specific with stages of buying, if you have specific ones you want to add, but at a minimum you'll want to differentiate the list questions in the rough order of when buyers ask them.

The Buyer Question Map isn't just for content creation. It is also the first step of a marketing content audit. By including all buyer questions, even those already answered by content, you will get a sense of where the content gaps are at. Note that we always start with the question in mind to avoid creating the wrong content. If a particular piece of content doesn't seem to fit the chart, you should question its value to your buyer!

Early-stage content typically revolves around the fact that the buyer doesn't even realize there's a problem, or they have an idea but they're not aware of how bad the problem is or can be. "Did you know that if you don't do *X* … or if you don't have *X* … you could get sued / be fined / lose out on *X*, *Y*, *Z*?" Early questions like those are all about letting them know there's a problem they need to address, whether they're aware of it or not, and just how big of a problem it is. The early stage content gives

> You want to engage them quickly and easily using content that piques their interest with information they really need or want.

them a *why* to drive their later action. Videos, podcasts, one-pagers, infographics—all of these types of content work well in the early stage, because you want to engage them quickly and easily using content that piques their interest with information they really need or want.

With early content, prospects aren't usually aware of the problem or your solution. Because of this they're not actively searching for a solution and certainly aren't ready to be sold anything. They're doing high-level research related to their career or industry. With all of this in mind, consider what types of content formats will fit your busy prospects. Early content is often industry or role best practice webinars, blog posts, and easy-to-digest, one-page guides. They have little commitment to your content, so you want to maximize its effectiveness by answering the question as quickly as possible. The benefit of webinars is that you can answer multiple questions at once!

Fire off your **midstage content** when your buyer recognizes the problem and is shopping for the answer. Ideally, they're trying to figure out how to select a vendor like you. "What criteria are important? How do I make a decision? There are so many vendors that do this; how do I know one from the other and who I can trust?" These are the types of questions you need to answer here. Midstage content typically utilizes comparison charts and documents that teach the specifics about criteria they'll use to evaluate vendors.

Consideration content benefits from a buyer who is actively researching solutions. Because of this commitment, they'll read and listen longer than they would in the awareness stage. Buyer persona research really comes in handy at this phase, as different personas often prefer different formats. Comparison charts in one-pager guides are very popular here because they allow a researcher to see difference between options at a glance. Industry analyst reports or summaries of them appeal to buyers by giving them consideration data from a third-party source.

Late-stage content is usually used for the sake of trust and reassurance. At this point they've hopefully chosen your solution and are looking for reassurances that they're making the right call. Late-stage content typically utilizes case studies and video testimonials from happy customers.

It's time to pull out all the stops on your late-stage content. This is the *decision* stage, and by its position, it's the last thing between a prospect being a customer. I usually recommend fixing up late-stage content first based on this. Multipage customer case studies and even success story videos are great for this stage. The best version of these references have a customer photo, title, years as a customer, and at least one strong quote. The work you did researching buyer personas can often be repackaged to create stunning late-stage content!

Meera Kothand, Author, MeeraKothand.com, "One Hour Content Plan"

The second column of our Buyer Question Map is "Answer to Question." As the name implies, here is where we work to actually answer the buyer's question or challenge. Try to summarize the information you have into one short answer. You can't write a novel, so just summarize what the core answer is. Make it as simple as possible. It's important for you to do this for two reasons: one, you want to make sure you actually know what the answer is, and two, it's going to inform your approach to the next column, which is the best way to deliver the answer.

The "Best Medium to Convey Answer" column is where things get creative. Is the best way to answer their question or challenge something visual? A picture speaks a thousand words, after all. Is that happy customer testimonial better? What about a well-respected case study? Or how about a nicely produced video? The possibilities are endless, and oftentimes there are multiple ways to answer a question.

GATING CONTENT TO CAPTURE LEADS

Once your content is created, it's time to make it available for your prospects. A landing page, also known as a squeeze or capture page, is one of the best tools for capturing a lead online. You may be surprised to learn that not everyone is on the same page with this topic, for whatever reason. To bring everyone together, I've found the best thing to do is to get in agreement with some definitions.

Brian Massey is a conversion scientist who, along with Joel Harvey, heads up the marketing think tank and consultancy firm, Conversion Sciences. I had the pleasure of interviewing Brian on the podcast, and I really enjoyed my time with him and learning about his methods. He has a great personality, lots of energy, and he was literally drinking his coffee out of a laboratory beaker!

Brian defines a landing page as a single-minded page that's as dead set on keeping the promise made by an ad, link, or email as it is on getting the visitor to take action. I love the clarity that definition provides, but let's chop it up into a few bits, shall we?

> **Landing page:** A single-minded page that's as dead set on keeping the promise made by an ad, link, or email as it is on getting the visitor to take action.

Single-minded page: "You had one job." Have you seen this meme? There's a picture of a sign hung upside down, a traffic lane painted askew, or some other simple task done so badly that it makes you question everything you know about people. Similarly, a landing page has one job: to get the person to take action. In a B2B sense, that action is typically converting to a lead, which we'll cover below.

It's important to call out single-minded, because this is the principle that I see violated the most. Brian calls it out too. Your homepage is *not* a good landing page. I absolutely hate seeing a paid ad go right to your homepage. Why's that? Because it's not single-minded. Your homepage, more than any other page on your site, has the most options available to the visitor. When humans are browsing the web, we're like dogs and cats. Yes, all of us. Let's own up to it. We had one purpose, but then … *squirrel*! We're easily distracted, so human psychology suggests that we make things easier on our visitor. By the time you get to a landing page—and we'll talk about how you get there next—it should be singularly focused on the call to action you need to take.

Let's look at an example. A lot of people, including myself, love Amazon. They have a great site, and we can learn so much from them. I want you to try an experiment. Add something to your shopping cart, and then click the "checkout" link. The very next page you get to—does it have frills? No! Navigation is removed, links to other things are gone—every pixel on that page is urging you forward. It's telling you, "Buy … buy … continue … you'll be *fine*!" It's as single-minded as they come. In a B2B world, to be a single-minded landing page, you encourage the completion of a form and nothing else. When we are

THE HARD CORPS MARKETING SHOW

EPISODE #012

Rebecca Lieb, Founding partner and analyst, Kaleido Insights, "Unleashing Atomic Content Strategy"

designing these pages for our customers, we recommend removing navigation.

Landing pages are critical for capturing new leads, and marketing automation increases their efficiency tenfold. Every landing page needs a call to action. This could be signing up for a webinar, downloading a whitepaper, signing up for an audit—the sky's the limit! But there needs to be an action that the page is driving you to complete. Some companies have big arrows pointing to the form that stands between you and the content you've been promised. Brian Massey has a whole architecture of testing that we'll highlight later in the testing chapter. (Give him a shout for optimizing your campaigns. He's definitely one of the best.)

STRATEGIES FOR OPTIMIZED LANDING PAGES

One marketer shared with me that his CEO hates forms, so they don't have any. They also don't have any leads coming in! Some vendors say all forms should be removed, and typically this is followed by replacing them with another kind of form, like a chat box. I hate *certain* kinds of forms. Long, obtrusive forms asking stupid, confusing, or personal questions are a pain in the ass to everyone, and they should *always* be avoided. With that said, let's look at the kinds of forms that you should use.

When we talked about the core of marketing automation, progressive profiling is the part that has earned *capture* a spot in the core values. *This* is the thing, and many people aren't taking advantage of it yet. When you place a form on a landing page using marketing automation systems like Pardot, they have the ability to dynamically change the form. It's amazing! It unlocks several different strategies for optimizing the experience and conversion rate for your prospects.

A few months ago, I was going through a website, and the contents sounded good. I was interested in the service, but the form asked a couple of questions that I really didn't want to fill in: personal salary, homeowner status … pretty personal stuff for a "first date!" I reluctantly completed them and went to another page to download a different piece of content. The form on the second page asked the same questions again! It was even more frustrating the second time, and I ended up leaving the site altogether. We know from the research that reducing fields increases conversions, so why ask a question twice?

The good news is that marketing automation systems like Pardot automatically remove a question from a form if it already knows the answer. So, by default, your forms are going to be more efficient if you already know something about someone, especially if they're coming back for a second or third time.

The next step beyond this is to use progressive profiling. Using this feature, you can restrict the form to asking a limited number of questions each time. One great way to leverage this tech is to not to ask for a phone number until you know your prospect's email address. The result of this simple strategy is that your initial form won't come on too strong by asking for a phone number right away. The next form that a prospect completes will have the phone number field, and since you're not asking too much, these get completed much more often.

Email is the most important question to ask, and on most forms it's required. Remember, we're moving from a strategy of "get all the answers up front" to nurturing people. That means we need to provide them with content and get them to fill out multiple forms along the way. In order to do that, we're going to need to get their email, of course. The great news is that, even though it's required, the best marketing automation tools have the ability to auto-populate the email address.

It's a barter, not a qualification. Don't forget that a landing page is a barter. If your content is breaking the rules we discussed, and your forms are asking too many questions, you won't find many takers for the exchange. In fact, you'll get what most violators get: lots of sales pitches and students doing research (i.e., not the leads you're looking for).

Andy Crestodina, Cofounder and CMO, Orbit Media Studios, "The Content Strategy EXPLOSION"

There is a myth that a long form prequalifies prospects. While it's true that some people may desperately need your thing and will fill out your stupid form, most people aren't at that stage, and you won't catch them filling it out. Remember this is a new strategy and a new approach, one that requires tact and patience.

Putting it all together: The tenants of gated content marketing can be summarized in three important steps. Keep these principles top of mind at all times when strategizing your approach:

- Consistently offer valuable and relevant content in your marketing.
- Deliver on that promise with tailored landing pages.
- Use marketing automation to dramatically increase the effectiveness and efficiency of the capture form on the landing page.

With these strategies active, it's time to utilize marketing automation to nurture your buyers with helpful emails!

CHAPTER 7

NURTURING YOUR BUYERS

CSI Question Number Five: Do you nurture your buyers in separate, relevant tracks?

If you google "What is email nurturing?" you'll get hundreds of videos on YouTube telling you *how* to build it. But your question remains, "What strategy should I take with them? What are the best practices?" Everyone's talking about how to build without considering what you should build in the first place.

It's no wonder, then, that many of those who have activated these features in their marketing automation aren't actually doing it right.

WHY IS NURTURING SO CRITICAL?

Technically speaking, you just spent all this money on capturing a new lead, and if you've done your work correctly and nailed the first four steps of the CSI, you're set up for success to do just that. But those steps alone won't close the deal. Specifically, in the last CSI, we set up progressive profiling, which only asks a few questions each time a prospect completes a form engaging with our content. This creates the need for additional engagement, and we need a way to do that.

THE HARD CORPS MARKETING SHOW

EPISODE #031

Sangram Vajre, Chief evangelist and cofounder, Terminus: Account-Based Marketing, "Mastering Account-Based Marketing"

The second thing that's happening is the few promising leads that do slip through the cosmic filter that Sangram Vajre talked about on my podcast are not typically ready to buy right now. In many circles this is known as the "danger zone." Queue up the *Top Gun* soundtrack in your mind for this next part.

Hop in the sales cockpit with me. A lead comes in, and we call them right away. We have a few calls with them, and it seems like what we're selling is a good fit for everyone. Then on our latest call, the prospect says, "You know, hey, this is all great, but … " (oh no, it's coming) "we're not ready right now." Uh-oh. "We need to do *X*, *Y*, and *Z* first." Then comes the "Call me in six months. We'll be ready then." Now, was that the truth, or was it a superpolite buyer who doesn't want to reject you outright? You have no idea, so you set a reminder for yourself in your CRM to call them again in six months.

Six months later, you call them and hear, "Oh, hi. Yes, we purchased from your competitor a few months ago." What? Just because they told you to call them in six months, there's no requirement for a buyer to actually wait that long. If they're ready early and you're not top of mind, they may begin their research elsewhere. This is the danger zone, my friends. The good news is, we're going to take control of the situation in this chapter, and you'll be the one they call when they're in your competitor's danger zone.

If they're ready early and you're not top of mind, they may begin their research elsewhere. This is the danger zone, my friends.

If there's one thing we can learn from Tom Cruise doing the 4G inverted dive with a MiG-28, it's that we need to expect the unexpected and plan for the long game in B2B. When we utilize the term B2B, what we're really talking about is the considered or the complex sale. A considered sale is a decision that often involves more than one person. As a result, B2B sales take more time and typically cost a lot more money than selling a candy bar or a pair of running shoes to an individual (B2C). And that's exactly why nurturing is so critical.

WHAT IS NURTURING?

We know that it's important to nurture your buyers, but what is nurturing really? Let's take a step back from marketing for a second. When you think of the word *nurture* or *nurturing* by itself, what comes to mind? Nurturing reminds me of mothers and babies. Dads get their snuggles, sure, but there is a special magic between a mother and her child. She cares for that little love nugget, no matter how many times she wakes her up in the middle of the night. Every twist or turn in life is a chance for a lesson to grow. And she's protective. We all know the adage to never get between a mother bear and her cub!

Nurture: To care for and encourage the growth or development of.

Google the definition of *nurturing*, and you'll find this: "To care for and encourage the growth or development of." I love the simplicity of this definition because it absolutely applies to our use in marketing. Let's tie the definition into our marketing initiatives and drip campaigns.

First, break down the definition into its two parts:

- Care for
- Encourage the growth or development of

"Care for." This isn't just some fuzzy part of the definition we toss out; it's actually more important than we think. In the case of mothers and babies, babies need love and to be held. They actually die if they're not held and loved. I shudder at that thought. Caring for our prospects is critical to nurturing too.

The emails we're sending need to have their interests at the heart of the communication. This means we're sending helpful content that alleviates their pain and helps them with their challenges.

At Cheshire Impact we have three core values: We Care. We Have Fun. We Get Things Done. The caring value is critical to how we operate, because it informs our decisions. When deciding between A and B, we weigh the choices against our core values. Does either option violate our values? If not, which one exemplifies them? Likewise, we should pay attention to caring in the definition of nurturing our buyers because the emails we're sending need to have their interests at the heart of the communication. This means we're sending helpful content that alleviates their pain and helps them with their challenges. Programmatically sending them sales pitches? That violates caring for them; therefore, it isn't nurturing.

"Encourage the growth or development of." The encouragement piece has four components:

- Helpful content
- Invites to webinars/events
- Links to articles
- Education of your buyer

Most marketers are doing everything but what I've just described. Nurturing through caring and encouraging growth/development is a simple standard that we've missed. Understanding the definition of nurturing helps us keep our heads up and keep the buyer at the forefront of our activities. And like a lot of things in life, this authentic, caring approach is actually the most successful.

Sales has been nurturing their buyers since the first B2B transaction that occurred. Many of them miss the definition of nurturing like we have in marketing, but the really good salespeople are amazing nurturers. In sales, the goal is to check in with your prospect at a pace that matches their need and continually offer more information to move them closer to a purchase.

Susan Baird, Senior business consultant, Cheshire Impact, "What Marketing Can Learn from the Heart of a Teacher"

When I was shopping for a marketing automation platform, I was in a baby state myself with the new technology. Many reps inundated me to death with data and pushy sales speak. My contact at Pardot was much more understanding. I got the sense he cared because the content he sent me was on point, helpful, and not overwhelming. (Come to find out, much of the content I received from his email address wasn't even from him! But we'll talk more about that later.)

Moving forward, when we talk about nurturing in a marketing sense, we're going to add *automated* to the textbook definition of nurturing. What I mean by that is that nurturing is automated care and encouragement of the buyer toward making a purchase. After all, the goal of marketing automation is to automate. It is to care at scale.

WHAT NURTURING IS NOT

Oh, yes, I'm rubbing my hands together ready to pounce on this one! Rant: ready, aim, fire!

It's said that we learn more from our failures than our successes. It's certainly true, and one of the best ways to clarify what nurturing is exactly is to discuss what it *isn't* and why.

Newsletters ain't it. They're a status quo and safe option, yet most people don't read them. We did all that work to understand our buyers in the first CSI, so why show them all this content at once that they don't really care about? When we do that, we come across as being very general and uninteresting, and the engagement with the content is extremely low. The other challenge with newsletters is they get harder to do the longer you do them.

I once wrote for a travel and activities magazine called *New*

Hampshire To Do. Now, New Hampshire is a great state, but it's not that big. So while at the start, our monthly articles were covering cool seacoast activities, fun hikes, and a lot of "You should all come visit New Hampshire … it's an awesome place!" type content, a few years later we were down to doing articles on model train museums and random cafés in small, rural towns.

Typically, with newsletters, the best content is created early on. So when marketing departments are looking to share B2B content, the most inspired writing happens at the beginning. You're on fire, and the content you're writing is exactly what your buyer needs to hear. But, unfortunately, the lead who gets on the list eight months later has missed all that juicy content and is stuck with your model train content. The good stuff doesn't get repeated, because you don't want the first group to reread it. By design, the quality decreases until you stop doing it or you leave for another position. The idea behind marketing automation nurturing is to take your best content and build it into an evergreen nurture campaign.

Evergreen means it doesn't expire. An example of evergreen content for marketing might be something like, "Five Things Nurture Campaigns Are Not!" (Psst, you're reading about one of them right now!)

Evergreen content gets its name from evergreen trees. Where I live in New Hampshire, the fall foliage is beautiful, and once all of the leafy trees shed their leaves, the green needles of the pine trees really stand out. They will keep their green throughout the long winter.

In a similar way, content that is evergreen keeps its value to your buyers all year. Unlike a newsletter, it's timeless. No matter what month a prospect receives the content, it addresses a problem or challenge they're having. A good example of evergreen content would be one-pagers that explain how you address certain customer pain points, customer success stories, and any content that doesn't expire. The importance of evergreen content is that you can build nurture campaigns that continue to educate your buyers long after you first set them up. This means you'll be adding to them, and your nurture campaigns will grow to cover the majority of the length of your sales cycle.

When set up properly, marketing automation will deliver a sequence of your best content to each buyer on their own timeline. If I complete a form today, I get your nurture email. Someone completing the same step will get that same first email. It's like a customized personal campaign, and it crushes newsletters in engagement, education, and results by encouraging buyers toward that sale!

Monthly campaigns are also very status quo. I've been there and, unfortunately, a lot of us still are. The best content sent manually might be nurturing but it's not automatic, so it doesn't fly here. The point of automation is to create paths that your buyers are sorted into automatically, and then send them content tailored to their interests. Instead of spending your time tactically executing each month, you spend it creating even better content to help out your different buyer personas.

Sales offers aren't nurturing either. Not only does spam violate the caring rule, it doesn't work and will most likely elicit an "unsubscribe" from that prospect.

Autoresponders. Remember the danger zone? We can't wait for someone to signal that they're out of it. Securing good leads requires someone to take an action in order to receive an action. We're not talking about when a form is completed and a system sends out an automatic email. We're talking about automatic responses from your marketing or sales team to your prospects.

In the past, web leads would come directly through the site to your front door, and it was up to you to figure out if they were hot, cold, warm, freezing, awesome, or junk. But with systems like Pardot, these same leads are evaluated and nurtured (i.e., sent regular, personal messages offering value), so sales isn't wasting as much time chasing leads down dead ends.

Gyi Tsakalakis, President, AttorneySync, "Marketing Attorney Talks GDPR"

CORPORATE VS. PERSONAL EMAILS

Fancy, corporate, "marketing emails" with lots of graphics are great for official announcements, invites to events, and autoresponders, but they're not great for creating a more personal tone.

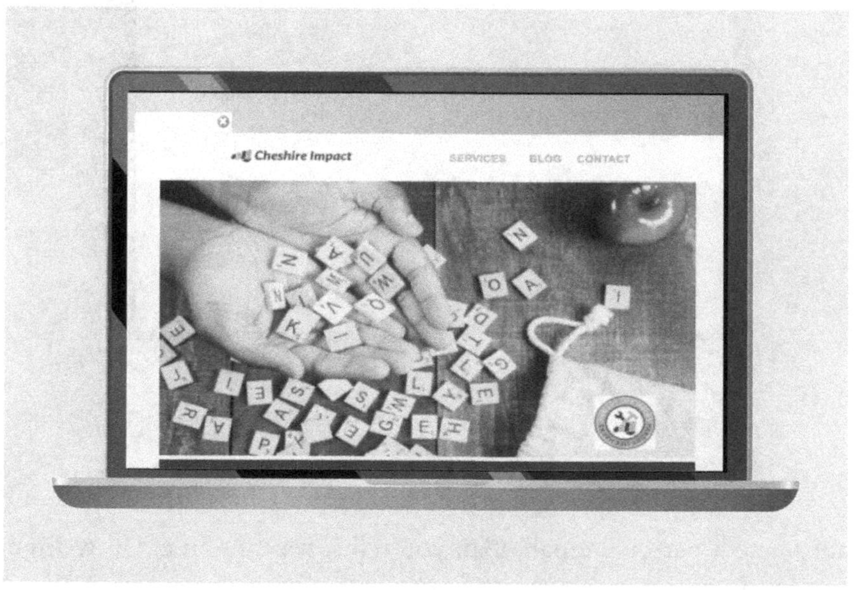

Personal emails get higher click-through rates, are read more often, and engage more leads. This is because they don't signal that they're junk or corporate communications like many emails today. When viewing our inboxes, we all tend to delete the junk before settling in to reading the rest. With this in mind, it's important to get it right at first glance.

Personal emails look like the sender hit "Compose New Message" and started typing. Take a second and go look at your inbox. Do you see any personal emails? Do you see any graphics-laden, corporate emails? The personal email has plain text, and it's usually pretty short. We're not writing Elizabethan love letters to each other anymore, unfortunately. They're usually pretty short and direct. What do they always tend to have at the bottom of a personal email? A signature with contact details and sometimes a company logo.

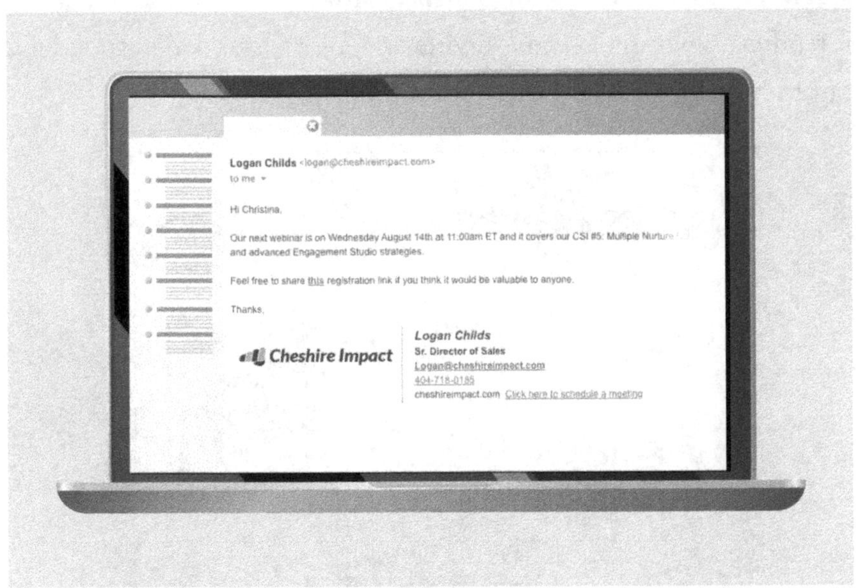

Look at the message from Logan to Christina; this is an automated, personal email. Can you tell it was not an email written specifically for Christina?

PERSONAL EMAILS	CORPORATE EMAILS
Short	Can be longer
Contain text until signature	Heavy use of graphics
Casual subject lines	Formal subject lines
From a person	From a company or team

Each email style has its purposes and can be used in your nurture campaigns. The most important thing to remember is to avoid blending the two styles. Personal emails are short, contain text until the signature, have casual subject lines, and are from a person. Corporate emails are heavy in the use of graphics (including a logo at the top), can be longer, have formal and detail laden subject lines, and come from a company or team. Imagine that there is a gigantic fence in between these two styles.

To gain maximum effectiveness, choose what kind of email you want to design and then stick to it. Every time you borrow from the other style, you violate the style expectations and reduce the effectiveness of *both* styles in the future!

NURTURING STRATEGY

High-level planning for Pardot nurture campaigns circles around whom you are sending to and what they will receive. Who are the people we are sending to? What are we going to send? Why are we sending it? When are we going to send it? Those are the questions to ask when building the content of your nurture campaign.

A great planning tool for your nurturing is the Buyer Question Map we completed earlier when auditing and creating our content:

STAGE	QUESTION(S) ASKED	ANSWER TO QUESTION	BEST WAY TO ANSWER
EARLY	How does this work?	XXXXXX	XXXXXX
MID	Whom are you competing against?	XXXXXX	XXXXXX
LATE	Does it work? How hard is it to implement?	XXXXXX	XXXXXX

Let's look at how a nurture campaign's content should transition through the different buying stages.

Early stage. Content in this "awareness" stage often addresses unaware prospects who either don't know there's a problem or have experienced related pain but are unsure of the cause. The content delivered early in your nurture campaign should be designed to educate your buyer and make them aware of the challenges you can help them solve.

Middle stage. The middle stage is often called "consideration," and the content delivered from nurture emails should reflect this. At this stage your buyer is aware of the problem and is seeking a solution to it. You're typically the solution, and content will help separate you from the other options.

Late stage. In the final stage we're educating and encouraging our buying to make a decision. The best email copy and content to deliver will back up their choice of your company. Case studies and success stories get a lot of engagement at this point.

There are different types of nurture campaigns that can be done as well.

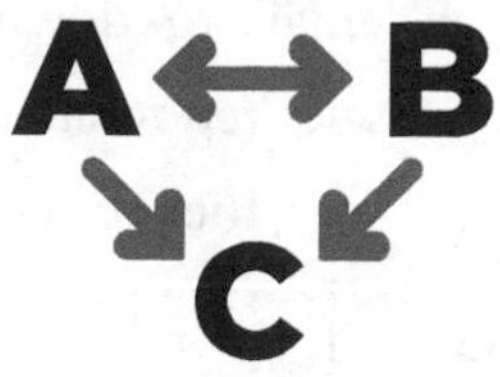

Triangle Nurture. A triangle nurture provides for two marketing assets that prospects can engage with that both lead to the same completion action. For example, I carried out this same nurture before where A was a demo, B was a case study, and C was a white paper. If a visitor came to the site that hosts the online demo (A) or they filled out a form to access the case study (B), then an email was sent from the solution architect I was working with at the time, David, with a "call to action" to download the white paper (C). Almost everyone that received the email from David clicked on the email to access the white paper, and David started getting a lot of email responses, providing direct engagement with potential buyers.

Linear Drip. The linear drip campaign has prospects move along your marketing assets in a linear format with a beginning, a middle, and an end. It can be thought of as a catchall. For example, A is a webinar recording, B is a white paper, and C is a case study. Every prospect that enters the drip campaign by filling out the form to access the webinar recording will then move on through the drip campaign by receiving an email to download the white paper, followed by an email from a sales rep to check out a case study once they download the white paper.

Samantha Stone, Founder and CMO, Marketing Advisory Network, "Unleash the Power of Quality Content"

Everyone moves through the drip campaign at their own time. For example, Bob could fill out a form to access the webinar recording, which automatically adds him to the drip campaign's list. Another prospect, Vicki, accesses the webinar recording four months later and is also added to the list to move through the same drip campaign. The drip campaign becomes evergreen, as in, it does not expire. It will always be relevant.

3-2-1 Drip. A 3-2-1 drip campaign is a novel approach to nurture design that I first learned from Mathew Sweezey , marketing thought leader and head of marketing insights at Salesforce. He poses the question: When it comes to nurturing, why make the people who are most ready to buy wait for your late-stage content? These late-stage prospects are waiting to see pricing, competition comparison, and case studies. The 3-2-1 drip strategy flips the order of your nurturing content to serve up late-stage content first. This addresses the needs of those looking to make a decision now. It's followed by mid- and early-stage content.

Remember that the ultimate purpose of nurture content is to inform, educate, and build relationships. Equipped with a solid understanding of nurturing and the market-leading strategies to execute it successfully, you're ready to use marketing automation to care about your buyers at scale!

SECTION III

ALIGNMENT PHASE

Welcome to the next phase of the Cheshire Success Index and your journey on maximizing marketing automation! In the previous two phases, we laid the groundwork for focused and accountable marketing to a specific audience. We then created landing pages and nurture campaigns to drive our leads forward. Many of them are now beginning to show signs that they're ready to talk to our sales team. The Alignment Phase has two critical elements to it, and they're completely geared around packaging up and delivering awesome leads, wrapped in a bow of insightful information, to our internal customer: sales!

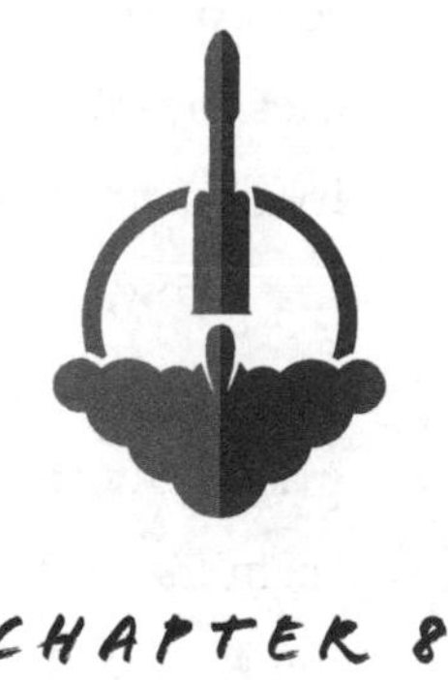

CHAPTER 8

SALES ALIGNMENT & ENABLEMENT

CSI Question Number Six: Is your sales team trained and actively using marketing automation inside your CRM?

Many moons ago, I was interviewing at a tech company to be their marketing manager. As part of the process, they wanted me to chat with a few of their sales directors. To this day, I remember what one particular sales leader shared rather matter-of-factly with me: "I think sales and marketing should always hate each other." That is crazy!

Finger-pointing, credit hoarding, and harsh politicking can easily emerge in organizations where their sales and marketing teams exist in separate systems with siloed data and processes. However, this is changing for many companies that adopt marketing automation strategies. This is seen often with start-ups and the SMB market that can be and are nimbler, with teams built on marketing ops roles vs. the sales and marketing siloed positions of the past. The marketing tool is now connected to the sales tool (CRM), bringing the possibility of a single process and unified data.

> The marketing tool is now connected to the sales tool (CRM), bringing the possibility of a single process and unified data.

Now, more than ever, B2B is a team sport, especially in large enterprises where the focus is on building "centers of excellence" and streamlining tech, process, and training. In order for our team to score by closing a deal, marketing needs to carefully plan and orchestrate in collaboration with sales. This introduces a different group with a strange language and culture. After all, salespeople have their own ways that differ from marketers.

Yes, sales can act like aliens from Mars. They can also be amazingly fun to work with. One story that comes to mind was when my team and I were invited by the VP of sales at our biggest partner to a join them in a sales celebration dinner at a very fancy steakhouse.

The dinner was incredible, but it wasn't until after our meal I learned that this sales leader had a special kind of calling card for ending business dinners. Several waiters with white gloves came out holding silver trays with a countless number of filled shot glasses on them! They passed one out to every single salesperson, as well as different partners and VIPs the leader had invited. We all had one gigantic "cheers" at the end of the night, and it was awesome. For all the slack we give to sales, they can be a lot of fun!

As marketers, we often experience a different type of environment. A lot of the time, marketers are sitting behind a computer writing campaign copy; sending emails; studying trends by piecing together data from multiple data points, tools, and resources; and preparing for an upcoming trade show. Other departments, including sales, aren't usually aware of this work unless we're deliberate about sharing it internally.

Understanding what each function actually does goes a long way in aligning marketing and sales. I highly recommend that everyone, marketers or any other position, get some sales experience by shadowing a fellow team member, or even stepping into the realm of sales during an event!

Early on in my professional career, I had the opportunity to work in a sales role for a tuxedo rental company. The insights were countless, and it was an awesome experience. My job was to show up, throw on a tux they had tailored just for me, and then get leads while standing in front of a booth at a trade show. This wasn't just any kind of trade show, though. These were bridal shows!

Tal Paperin, VP of business development, KSW Solutions, "Global Sales Fundamentals"

They would open the doors, and a flood of soon-to-be brides would come storming through looking at flower vendors, location vendors, photographers, and yes, tuxedos. Our job was to answer questions, calculate a custom show floor discount, and ultimately get them to sign up to check out tuxes at one of many local stores. It was not always easy, believe me. My offer was often turned down, which is something that sales has to frequently overcome.

Being challenged or even rejected in person is a whole lot more intense than through a web campaign. While each role has their importance, let's make sure we don't discount the work done by sales, but rather use that experience to sharpen the focus and direction of a nurture stream that marketing develops. This allows for gathering specific data points that directly increase the conversion of a qualified lead to a sales-engaged contact, and eventually to an opportunity won.

Now, just as we're confused about what sales often does, sales is often just as unclear on what we do in marketing! I once had a conversation with a seasoned sales leader who had run large sales teams. While planning out lead generations for the upcoming year, we were working together and collaborating, and I was thinking with a marketing mind about lead sources and campaigns. After I shared some of my ideas, I could tell from his response that the sales leader didn't put much stock in the approach, or even the concept of marketing itself. He preferred instead to have the sales reps source all their leads on their own. He actually told his team, "Look, guys, you need to hit your quota no matter what. These leads from marketing, yeah, they're just bonus. They're not an excuse, so do your job."

This is not an entirely unexpected thing for an experienced sales leader to say, because this has very much been how B2B businesses have operated in the past. With marketing automation having been generally available for over a decade, these out-of-date attitudes are thankfully becoming fewer. When it comes to alignment, it isn't enough for marketing to simply have the technology. The sales team needs to be aware of the information marketing automation captures as well as the relevant functionality that can make their jobs more efficient. They need to know how they play a role in identifying key data points and how it all aggregates in one place, the CRM. This is first accomplished with great training, which starts the spark of marketing and sales working together.

THE START TO A BEAUTIFUL RELATIONSHIP

With our team's collective experience of more than two thousand Pardot implementations, I am often asked about the most important part of deploying marketing automation. Despite the long list of flashy deliverables, one of the most impactful experiences is our Pardot training for sales. No matter what the relationship was prior to the training, it's guaranteed to create "aha moments" in the minds of the sales professionals in attendance. More often than not, everyone leaves the fast-paced meeting energized and eagerly anticipating all the cool things marketing is planning to build with sales.

There's nothing magic about what is covered. No trust falls or sweat lodges are utilized. It's simply presented as information that will directly assist sales in closing more deals. Whether the team at Cheshire Impact is presenting this information or you are, there are critical elements to cover. Let's review the best practices of the Pardot training for sales.

I know, I know, I can already hear you: "Sales in CRM! No, we are not training sales to use your marketing automation technology." Don't worry. Sales should continue to work in the CRM and be able to view the information they need to see from marketing right from there. All of this is possible because, for the first time in many organizations, the marketing automation software is now directly connected to the sales software (CRM).

SELLING IT TO SALES

If we take a twelve-thousand-foot view of marketing automation, **capture**, **nurture**, **automate**, and **report** are the pillars. We had a whole chapter on this subject, but we want to give sales a kind of aerial view of marketing automation, through a sales lens. They don't need to know the ins and outs, just the basics of marketing automation's purpose and how it can help them.

Capture: It's good for sales to know that you have magic forms that can capture more data. Later you'll be collaborating on just what type of questions you'd like asked and answered.

Nurture: When you're sending an email that looks like it's from the sales rep, what does it say and why? If you don't have this conversation with sales first, you'll get a lot of defensive pushback. Their relationship with their prospects is critical to sales, and they pay a lot of attention to anything that affects it.

Automate / Lead Flow: Sales needs to know at what point you're sending a lead over. What happens if they want to send a lead back? What's expected? The information that's captured can be discussed here too.

Report: It's good for sales to know you have the ability to track ROI based on information they enter (and the opps they close) so you can do more of the things that get them the best leads.

Information: Simply put, marketing automation captures an amazing amount of information about the buyer and their activities, which will make it easier and faster for sales to close their deals. But let's look at the kind of information we should pass on to sales.

Profiling Data: Remember that we're capturing lots of info via progressive profiling on forms in the earlier CSI. This information can be demographic, firmographic, or even buyer intent and qualification data, which we'll talk more about in the next section.

Buyer Activity: Any and every interaction a user has with you needs to be recorded. In the end, you'll know what they've done and when. Marketing cares about the aggregate typically, while sales cares about the exact buyer and their behavior. Are they engaged? What are they researching? That type of information is very useful to sales. You also don't want to come across as being too invasive, and we'll talk about how to avoid being creepy later.

Garner White, Sales manager and RVP, Salesforce, "Sharpening Your Sales Strategy"

BEST APPROACHES TO TRAINING

Champions first: Train the sales managers and team leaders first. Getting their buy-in is vital to the success of aligning marketing and sales teams. Also, "sell" them on the technology. Oftentimes they have never heard why the organization made the move in the first place, and we've all been in companies that make decisions that seem wild or careless and no one explains the purpose to us. When that happens, it's frustrating, confusing, and hard to adapt to the changes.

> We've all been in companies that make decisions that seem wild or careless and no one explains the purpose to us. When that happens, it's frustrating, confusing, and hard to adapt to the changes.

A great example of champions-first training came from a recent Salesforce Engage training project with a large financial services client.

With hundreds of sales reps across many offices, group training typically occurs during their annual sales kickoff event. For a few days in their new fiscal year, the entire sales organization meets on site. In order to maximize the training time we had with the sales teams, we executed a champions-first program by training sales managers first. The managers received a train-the-trainer type of instruction. Even though we would do the initial training for their teams, it was important that the managers understood the best practices. It was also important that the managers "bought in" to the value of using Engage. This would ensure that they encourage their teams to use the tool and take advantage of its benefits long after the training we did later with their teams.

Show an example / tell a story: People forget facts, but they'll remember the story! When I lead the training, do you think people remember the name of a drop-down box or whether it's called nurturing, drip, or automation? Not always. And that's okay. They don't need the terminology as much as they need to utilize the methods and take action. Pro tip: Create easy-to-read visual tables to pin up in offices or cubicles that refer to the essential drop-downs used for triggers or new processes to hand out after story time is over.

Stories are also a way of teaching without exerting a power position. I'm not telling you what to do or claiming that I have the experience to do that in the first place. I'm only telling you something that happened to me, how I handled it, and the result I got. I trust that you can draw your own conclusions from it and take the appropriate action.

One story that I find gets a sales rep's attention comes from our example of nurturing in action from the previous chapter. If you recall that situation, a prospect named Christina had previously told her sales rep, Logan, that she wasn't ready to buy and to call her back in six months. Logan not only set a reminder on his CRM but also added Christina to a nurture campaign. It sent her a helpful nurturing email every month from his address. This kept Logan top of mind with Christina, and sure enough, she was actually ready after three months. Seeing Logan's email, she replied to it and asked when he was free to do a sales call.

For those in sales who are constantly trying to ask and get onto their prospects' calendars, to have a prospect ask for your availability is an amazing thing!

Jeremy Pound, CEO, RentScale, "Scaling Sales Teams"

Don't be creepy, though! "With great power comes great responsibility," says the famous quote, and that's exactly what we need to remember about marketing automation. Capturing data, automating personal emails, and the like can come off as a bit sneaky. For that reason, a key component of this training should involve warnings not to be creepy, as well as instructions on how to utilize this information. There are a few ways to do this.

Explicit and implicit actions: Filling out a form is giving you the information explicitly, just as is registering for a webinar or signing up for a white paper. This is an **explicit action** taken by the user. They filled out the form or signed up for the webinar, and you know about it. It's pretty sharp to know that they took an action unrelated to sales, and you're referencing it. It just shows that you're a world-class organization. That's totally cool. You can (and should) always reference explicit information and explicit actions that they buyer has taken.

Information you know about the buyer that they didn't personally tell you is an **implicit action**. This is the kind of information we learn from seeing that they attended the webinar they signed up for, or that they went to the pricing page yesterday and spent eight minutes there. Typically, we're talking about actions they took, but this can also be data you gathered from other sources. You never want to directly mention this kind of information, because, well, it makes you sound creepy. They'll want to clear their cookies and probably not talk to you again. All this does is hurt the relationship.

***Serendipity* approach:** Utilize marketing automation information by either stating the explicit action or use the *Serendipity* approach. I named the approach after the movie *Serendipity* that came out in 2001. In the romantic comedy, the main characters play a game of avoiding direct connection. Instead of swapping phone numbers, they decide to see if fate would bring them back together. Naturally, Hollywood brings them back together numerous times.

In much more practical terms, the *Serendipity* approach for using information captured by marketing automation attempts to create similar outcomes to the movie. This is done by giving credit to the fates for bringing a sales rep and prospect together with perfect timing, instead of sharing that it was because of marketing automation.

A good example of this would be when a sales rep saw that one of his strategic prospects was actively on his company's pricing page. (Yes, this is possible!)

If the rep has time, it would be a good idea to reach out to the prospect immediately, because they're actively engaged in research, and it would be less of an interruption to them.

When the prospect picks up the phone, could you imagine if the sales rep said something to the effect of, "Hey, Jennifer! I see you're actively on our pricing page. In fact, I see you've been looking at it for something like five minutes and twenty-three seconds. Do you have a question about pricing?"

Hello, creep factor! Jennifer is likely going to be clearing her browser's cookies, and the sale is in jeopardy.

By contrast, the *Serendipity* approach would begin something more like: "Hey, Jennifer! I had you on my list today to connect and wanted to see if you were able to go to that webinar?"

I've been on these calls and often the prospect's response is, "What a coincidence! I was just doing some research and had a question … "

Hint at the road map: It's likely that when you are training your sales team and teaching them about all of the valuable information available to them, not everything is in place. That's okay! CSIs aren't built overnight, so it's important to end your training with what the teams can expect to see down the road, what features are currently working, and what will be available later.

When you share the collective stories and practical use of Pardot or your marketing automation tool with sales, they're going to get very excited. I've been in many boardrooms with sales executives who started out feeling very inconvenienced (and not shy to share it out loud) only to become strong advocates for marketing automation a few minutes in. Don't be surprised if they extend their schedules to be at the entire meeting.

While it's a good problem to have, an excited sales leader will also want the nurturing, implicit data capture, and the rest of the features ASAP. You can plan ahead for this by including a high-level plan for your intended rollout of marketing automation features in the training.

Encourage adoption: You know the old adage, "You can bring a horse to water, but you can't make him drink." You can bring a pancake to a child, too, but it doesn't guarantee he'll eat it. My son, Jon, comes to mind. It's all about those chocolate chips with him. Add those to a pancake, and he's very likely to polish off the whole thing. Likewise, don't forget when training sales that the goal here is to get sales teams to use and reap the benefits of having a marketing automation system. The whole goal is helping sales close more deals, of course, so a program that requires and encourages alignment as much as it does the tactical use of the technology is important.

John Barrows, Author, JBarrows Sales Training, "Thriving from the Evolution of Sales"

The best way to encourage sales's adoption of marketing automation is to train their leaders first with a champions-first training and then ensure that each training has as many success stories as possible. I've shared many stories in this book, and if you'd like more, definitely reach out to Cheshire Impact. You'll find that they're adoption ammunition!

Don't stop after the first training: Continue to sell the system internally nonstop. Remember to focus on your internal customer: sales. Share success stories of reps that have used the system to close deals, and watch other reps emulate them. Repeat the training and continue to message to sales leaders and the rest of the team when possible, sharing successes. Don't make this a one-and-done session.

For example, a sales manager for a client of ours would feature his top sales reps sharing recent wins with the tool during their daily stand-ups. Having successful reps share their use of the tool and its information has the double effect of both training and motivating adoption.

Feedback loops: Get feedback on what's working and what's not from the sales leaders and reps themselves. The feedback you get can be used to create a new nurture campaign, training slide, or even marketing campaign. Remember, they interact with your buyers every day!

With your sales team now actively finding value in your marketing and buyer activities and the tools exposed to them in their CRM, you'll have gotten their attention for the next CSI, which is all about getting them more of what they want: quality leads that are ready to buy!

CHAPTER 9

TWO-DIMENSIONAL LEAD RATING

CSI Question Number Seven: Do you separately rate your leads for activity and quality? (Two-dimensional lead rating)

Have you ever driven a car with one eye closed? (Please don't try that and blame this book for the outcome!) That second eye is what gives you depth. The military-grade night vision goggles I used in the marines used one camera to present the same image to both eyes on a lime-green screen. The result of wearing them is a world without depth, like playing a 2-D game on an original Nintendo system. Without depth perception it's much easier to run into and over objects, as it's harder to judge your distance to them.

What's crazy is that we're often forcing our sales team to play this same game with the leads we send. Even worse is that they often only have a single dimension in the form of a lead score to work with.

We're going to fix that in this chapter!

When I was working for that tuxedo sales company that I told you about in the last chapter, one of the most important lessons I learned as a sales rep was the importance and value of prioritizing my time. Those bridal shows lasted for only a couple of hours, during which I had to get as many sign-ups as possible. While discussing tuxedos, it was fun to hear from brides about their dreams and plans for their ideal wedding. Investing this time in potential customers was fun and proved worth it. It wasn't, however, worth trying to push someone who wasn't a good fit for our service or who was adamantly opposed to it. Watching fellow sales reps around me on the show floor, I realized that the best ones had not only mastered what to say and do, but how to identify the best potential buyers. In other words, they could spot the most qualified leads, in whom they would then invest most of their time. The best salespeople, I learned, are actually time-prioritizing champions.

It's important to know who fits so you can invest your time accordingly. You don't want to spend a lot of time with the wrong people. People who aren't a good fit, or who clearly are not interested at all, shouldn't get your time. If I'm going to spend five minutes talking to someone, they should be a candidate who is very likely to sign up.

Kasim Aslam, Founder and CEO, Solutions8, "Lead Gen Mastery"

In a salesperson's mind, chasing a lead requires a quick analysis of the time needed to pursue it and the likelihood and/or payoff of closing the deal. Traditionally, marketing has attempted to signal the relative importance of a lead through a lead score. Unfortunately, most marketers do it wrong, to the dismay and anger of sales reps everywhere!

LEAD SCORES GIVE MARKETING A BAD RAP

The traditional lead scoring model has tortured sales teams for years, because while the score is supposed to indicate how ready a lead is to buy, its misguided execution often means the scores don't align with what sales considers to be a qualified lead.

Most lead scoring systems are designed to award points to prospects based on the actions they take. Web page visits often get a point or two, while form completions and webinar attendance often garner fifty or more points. Additional workflows are often built to add points for countless other scenarios, including giving prospects points for attending a trade show or visiting certain high-value pages on the website. Some marketers even went beyond awarding points strictly for engagement activity and would boost scores based on demographic information such as industry or company size, or according to giving the "right" answers to presales questions on forms.

> Lead scoring, in its purest form, measures the engagement of your prospects.

Lead scoring, in its purest form, measures the engagement of your prospects. Each action they take corresponds to an amount that is awarded to their total score. Note this definition assumes that grading will be used and all measures of lead quality will be separately tracked by a lead grade.

Here's an example of lead scoring in action:

Jon is looking for a solution to a problem his company is experiencing. He clicks through to your site from Google and begins browsing. Each page on your site that he visits increases his lead score by 1 point. His first visit has included quite a bit of clicking! After visiting 12 pages, his lead score is 12. He then completes a form to get one of your downloadable strategy guides. Completing the form increases Jon's score by 50, bringing his total up to 62.

Let's say that immediately after completing one form, Jon was offered another, related piece of content. He visits the landing page for this newest content, giving him an additional point. Finally, Jon completes the form on this new page. His score has now jumped to 113.

If your automation rules were set up to assign all leads that have a lead score greater than 100, these actions would now trigger, and Jon would be assigned to a sales rep for follow-up.

I once worked with a client that had used every different method of incrementing scores of prospects in their marketing automation system, resulting in scores ranging from 4 to 4,000+. What conclusions can you possibly draw from that, other than that anyone with a score in the top 20 percent better either be a customer already or is probably an internal employee?

Here's an example of what I mean:

You're a sales rep at a company, and you've been tasked with calling the following leads. Whom do you call first?

George: Score 400

Tracy: Score 94

Elizabeth: Score 54

Philip: Score 512

Based on score, you'd have to answer Philip. "A prospect has a lead score of 512? Wow! This must be a hot lead! Drop everything!" So you focus your efforts on Philip, and after two weeks of trying to connect, he finally picks up the phone, and you discover that he's a student doing research for a class project. This explains why Philip clicked, opened, and downloaded everything he could find. He even attended a webinar!

That's just one scenario where the high score didn't reflect the quality of the lead, but it doesn't take too many times for a rep to get excited about a high score lead only to find out that he or she isn't a good fit before the rep stops trusting the lead score. That only fuels the rift that's defined by sales claiming marketing doesn't send them qualified leads, and marketing saying sales doesn't follow up on the highly scored leads it sends over.

JP Rinylo, Director of sales, Inverta, LLP, "Sales and Marketing Walked into a Bar"

LIKE OREOS & MILK

Scoring done right can be a valuable indicator. The problem is that it's only half of the equation. Like a peanut butter sandwich longing for jelly or an undunked Oreo, the lead score is only one side of the coin. The solution is a two-dimensional lead rating system, where a buyer's engagement is measured in one column, and their "fit" is evaluated in the second one.

Enter lead grading, which helps identify how closely a lead matches the qualifications of what sales considers to be their "ideal" customers. Separating the "quality" metrics that include demographic data like industry, company size, job title, etc. from the activity metric allows reps to see the whole picture and frees up scoring to be specific to activity or engagement. With the right strategic model, lead scoring measures how engaged a prospect is (i.e., how

> Score is how interested the prospect is in you, and grade is how interested you are in them.

many times they've clicked, registered, downloaded, taken favorable action, etc.). Lead grading measures how well a lead meets sales's qualification requirements.

One of the best ways I've heard this succinctly described is that "score is how interested the prospect is in you, and grade is how interested you are in them."

To illustrate this point, let's look back at the lead scoring challenge we failed earlier.

You're a sales rep at a company, and you've been tasked with calling the following leads. Whom do you call first?

George: Score 400, Grade B

Tracy: Score 94, Grade B

Elizabeth: Score 54, Grade A

Philip: Score 512, Grade F

How'd we do this time? Much better! Adding the second dimension of grade to indicate how well a prospect matches what we consider an ideal fit makes the choice clear. While Elizabeth hasn't clicked or downloaded as much as the other leads, she is the decision maker at an ideal company for our product. She is exactly the kind of lead that sales gets excited about and should be called first.

I kept the order of prospects the same between both examples and listed grade second to make it easier to compare experiences. When you implement a two-dimensional system in your own company, I recommend that sales reps sort their leads and contacts by grade first, and then by score. The resulting view in CRM for your sales team will look like this:

Elizabeth: Grade A, Score 54

George: Grade B, Score 400

Tracy: Grade B, Score 94

You'll see how much easier it is for sales to prioritize. They simply call down the list. They reach out to all of the grade A leads first, contacting the most engaged first. Then they call the Bs, reaching out to George before Tracy. Both of them are B-quality leads, but George has been more engaged in the process.

You'll also note that Philip is missing from this list. As a grade F lead, sales shouldn't even see him because he shouldn't be passed over to the team.

Done right, a two-dimensional scoring and grading model is a beautiful, beautiful thing. The sales team's process is so much more efficient, and marketing's reputation is boosted from delivering (and highlighting) those quality leads. Sales and marketing are aligned in defining what the ideal leads are, and everyone starts acting like they're on the same team.

However, to get these results, the sum is only as good as its parts. Now that we understand how lead scoring and grading work together, let's go through the most effective strategies for executing them individually.

SCORING STRATEGIES

The goal of lead scoring as a part of a grading and scoring combination is to identify how interested a prospect is in you. To this end, it's important to ensure that engagement points are awarded only for prospect activity and are never related to characteristics that define who they are. Those demographic characteristics must be relegated to the grading model, or you run the risk of giving double weight to things like a prospect's industry or job title by allowing it to boost both their score and their grade. Anything to do with who a prospect is, what company they work for, or how qualified they are must only affect the grade.

When it comes to how many points should be awarded for different actions in a lead score, it turns out that the actual point values don't matter as much as the preservation of the **action-work ratio**.

The number of points given for an action should be relative to the amount of work a prospect had to do to take the action. Opening an email takes little to no work on the part of a prospect. In many email apps, deleting the previous email may result in the opening of the next one in the queue. Clicking a link takes the movement of several muscles in a finger, worth a point or so. Browsing your website can similarly be rewarded, but it's not until a form is completed or a webinar is attended that the real points should be attributed.

And this brings up the second important factor in scoring based on the action-work ratio, the differences between scoring "big action" and "little action." First, there needs to be two levels of scoring. We divide these levels into either a "big score" or a "little score." An ideal ratio is to stay around fifty to one. So a big score would get fifty points, while a little score would get one to three points.

Second, the number of points awarded by either a big score or a little score must correlate with the amount of effort it takes a prospect to take an action. A link click or web page visit takes very little effort by a prospect. You'll often see a web page visit give one point for this very reason. Link clicks take an ever-so-slight increase in effort by the prospect. Their little finger had to click that mouse! Because of this, you'll often see scores of three points given to clicks.

I'm often asked why I don't give points for email opens. The action-work ratio answers this question. Oftentimes, an email open occurred simply from a previous email being deleted and automatically being displayed. Zero work by the prospect, zero points rewarded. That and the rate of email opens is one of the more dubious metrics to rely on!

Big score events are primarily form completions. Web-based chat conversations are on the rise, and a dialogue like this fits squarely into the big score category. In both cases, the prospect deliberately typed information and engaged with you.

The good news is that Pardot was designed with default scoring that meets the requirements of the action-work ratio. Translation: The default scoring can be left alone! In fact, I can count on two hands the times that the scoring actually needed to be overhauled based on unique conditions!

Nate Skinner, VP of product marketing, Salesforce, "A Trailblazer's Guide to ABM"

Once the marketing team determines a scoring benchmark, an automation rule can be set to push new leads who exceed the benchmark—and who have earned a grade higher than a C, for example—over to the sales team to review. I recommend making that benchmark score 100 to ensure that two big actions, such as forms, have occurred before a prospect is sent to sales. Completing two forms will allow us to capture the information we need to create a proper lead.

GRADING STRATEGIES

In the first CSI chapter, we talked about identifying your ideal buyer. This gets reflected here in the grading model, utilizing a range of grades between A and F. Grades are based on the cumulative number of characteristics that a prospect meets, which have been defined by sales as being shared by all of their top buyers.

At first, sales may struggle to define these characteristics, because their experience has enabled them to "know it when they see it." However, if they want marketing and Pardot to automate the process, sales has to specify which characteristics matter. If sales has trouble building the list, the opportunity data in the CRM should provide the historical context they need to find the criteria the best customers share.

What's tricky about building this list of criteria is reminding the team that the information needs to be something the marketing team can collect *before* their first conversation with them. Therefore, the questions need to focus on things that prospects will willingly share, such as industry, job title, company size, location, even role, and steer clear of more sensitive questions like budget or timeline. Answers to those sorts of questions may be more appropriate to learn in a personal conversation with the prospect.

One additional tip is to only include criteria that are related to pick-list fields with standardized values, rather than free-form text fields. It will make it much easier to automate the grading process and keep people from falling through the cracks because the grading rule didn't know what to do with a "strategic analytics evangelist" job title.

Another advantage of using standardized field values is that it might allow you to ask some of those more sensitive BANT questions in a way that allows prospects to provide a general indication without having to disclose specifics. For example, a question for timeline might be: "What's your project's timeline?" and the choices might be:

- No timeline
- Immediate project
- Doing research
- Project in nine months

This way, the prospect can give a general indication of how soon they're looking to make a purchase, or whether they want to make a purchase at all without having to commit to anything yet.

Lauren Mead, CMO, TimeTrade, "Alignment through Collaboration"

I'm mystified that more platforms haven't made two-dimensional lead rating a built-in feature like Pardot has. Other tools rate leads with stars and flames, but they generally indicate other qualities than quality. Regardless of the tool you use, ensure you've got two dimensions in your lead rating based on activity and quality.

Once you've started to properly grade prospects, it's important that you don't send Ds and Fs to sales; only send quality leads. You can build automation to ensure that D and F leads never get sent to sales. Eliminating the bad ones will help improve relations with sales, as you remove leads they're going to reject anyway.

Finally, I'll close this chapter with a reminder that grade and score must always be used together. Linking them is an awesome step toward aligning marketing and sales in your organization. You'll both be looking for the same type of lead and collaborating on getting them across the finish line!

SECTION IV

OPTIMIZATION PHASE

The last phase is the **Optimization Phase**. This is the point where we get to do most of our campaign testing as well as deploying the most advanced features in marketing automation. You have all the infrastructure built. The reporting is in place. The assets are in place. The landing pages, emails, nurturing campaigns—all of these are happening! Now it's time to optimize.

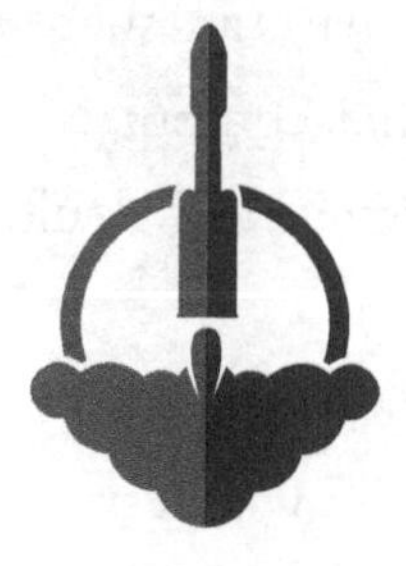

CHAPTER 10

A/B TESTING & OPTIMIZATION

CSI Question Number Eight: Do you test what messaging drives the most engagement in emails or landing pages?

"No plan survives first contact with the enemy." Have you heard that adage before? It's incredibly popular in both military and business circles, and it's attributed to a nineteenth-century Prussian military commander named Helmuth van Moltke. He wrote in 1880, "No plan of operations reaches with any certainty beyond the first encounter with the enemy's main force."

The good news for us is that we don't have to defeat anyone in battle, so what we're really talking about here is that our best-laid marketing automation plans will need adjustment as our buyers proceed through them.

As we look at our existing programs, several questions come to mind: Is it working? Which parts are successful? Which are not? What content is crushing it? What content is a miss? All these questions could be simplified into one: How could we make this better? It's time to optimize!

Whole books are written on this topic, so in this chapter, we're going to start by talking about why testing is important and highlight the challenges that may have prevented actionable testing in the past. Then we'll talk about what should be tested, and then how to test. Finally, we'll talk about the most common testing trap and how to avoid it!

WHY EVERYONE SHOULD TEST

Optimizing your marketing is one of the most exciting aspects of the profession. There are amazing improvements hidden in every marketing campaign, waiting to be discovered through intentional, well-planned optimization.

> There are amazing improvements hidden in every marketing campaign, waiting to be discovered through intentional, well-planned optimization.

Something as simple as a landing page is a perfect target for testing. One manufacturing client of ours was able to nearly double the amount of conversions by enacting several best practices. They changed the image at the top of the page to show their product in use from the user's perspective, simplified and focused the headline, and reduced the overall size of the form on the page. They were smart and tested their new page against the current page. This ensured that if their changes went south, they could continue on with the old page.

This test led to amazing results! The conversion rate increased by 96 percent! Elsewhere, a generic image was replaced with a real-life image, resulting in a 37 percent increase in leads captured. Crazier still, an A/B test with cleaned-up copy, a changed picture, and the form above the fold resulted in over 200 percent in increases. Not all tests are winners. In fact, the average winner is one out of seven tests. But with the strategy and process in this chapter, you can raise that rate!

Joe Apfelbaum, CEO, Ajax Union, "Marketing Mojovation!"

"Marketing equals testing." That's a statement made to me by Joe Apfelbaum on my podcast. Joe is the CEO of Ajax Union and author of the book *Average Joe to CEO*, and he has a lot of great advice to marketers on the subject of testing. It's not about winners and losers, he says. Instead, it's about winners and learners. You have to keep learning, and if you don't, then you're not truly winning. You should always be testing and progressing. Stagnant strategies won't carry you into the future.

Plus, testing can be fun! It requires equal parts creativity and measurement. The arts and the sciences get their turn when it comes to optimization!

THE CHALLENGES TO SUCCESSFUL OPTIMIZATION

Unfortunately, when you ask a marketer about their optimization efforts, you're all too often met with a comment about a recent A/B test on email subject lines, or the answer is no testing at all. Why is this? There are a few reasons.

We're busy. Many marketers aren't optimizing because they're too busy. Get that monthly campaign out the door, rinse, and repeat. I've been there, and it's crazy. But automation, when it is fully deployed, will free up the time it takes to be devoted to optimization.

We're skipping ahead. If you haven't set up the tracking in the Foundational Phase, chances are likely you may not even be able to tell what is actually working. Similarly, if you haven't built out landing pages and nurture campaigns, there really isn't anything of substance to test.

We're confused. What should we test? Without a direction on where to start, we often resort to testing simple things like subject lines. Sometimes these little tests actually result in a win, which just compounds the problem because we have no idea why the test won. Without understanding of what we're testing and why, it's hard to get traction and move forward with our marketing.

STRATEGIC HIERARCHY FOR MARKETING OPTIMIZATION

The days of casual testing button colors and subject lines is over! As I mentioned earlier, I interviewed Brian Massey, who is known in marketing circles as "the Conversion Scientist" on the podcast. He is a managing partner at Conversion Sciences, a company that plans and runs hundreds of marketing tests for their clients. Not only does Brian wear a lab coat and drink coffee from a beaker, but he also shared with me a path that marketers should follow when deciding what to test!

Just like how the CSI gives us a path for maximizing marketing automation, a hierarchy for marketing optimization will ensure we test the things that areas that promise the biggest results first.

Value proposition: The most important thing to test is your value proposition. Just as our primary directive for content creation in CSI number four was creating content that is valuable and helpful to our buyers, this is the first step in our testing plan. Do the words and images we use in our emails, landing pages, content, and other communications accurately describe our value to the buyers? Specifically, how do we address the challenges and pain points they have?

A great way to remind yourself this concept is to make sure you store the WIIFM radio station to your car's presets or favorite the WIIFM playlist in your Spotify app. "WIIFM" stands for "What's in it for me?" The "me" in this case is your buyer. By remembering to tune into this mindset, we're challenging every marketing message with a no-nonsense question: Is this helpful to them? If I was a customer, would I find value in this message? Testing different value propositions and the wording specific to each is the best place to start!

Layout: You next want to test the physical layout of the assets you're creating to ensure they're getting your buyers' eyes to the value propositions you previously tested. Is the layout of the landing page highlighting the right points, or is it too busy and full of competing words? It's important to note at this stage that the most beautiful layout isn't always the one that does the job the best! As we learned from the button color story, lime green or some wild hue doesn't match the colors in your corporate style guide, but it may actually draw the attention better than anything else.

Daniel Burstein, Senior director of content and marketing, MECLABS Institute, "Conversion Testing Jedi Master"

Credibility: With value and layout tested, attention shifts to testing supporting items that boost your buyer's confidence in taking the next step. The credibility and authority of your brand and its message are important to test here. What thought leadership content and expert quotes best support my value proposition claim? Statistics can make an impact here, though use them sparingly or you'll risk information overload. Analysts reports and industry awards perform well here; just ensure you keep them up to date or risk looking like yesterday's news!

Social proof: After expert leadership, the next area to test is elements of social proof. Our buyers are asking themselves, "What do my peers think? What did they research? What do they value? What did they choose, and ultimately, were they happy with that decision?" One of the best demonstrations of happy customers comes from the WordStream website. Not only do they give the name of a happy client, they also put up their picture, the number of years they've been a customer, and a review they wrote. Test these designs and messages to see which ones best support your brand as a peer-approved decision.

Let's see how the hierarchy works by following a marketer at an organization like yours through the process. Elizabeth is a marketing manager at small but growing tech company. Their ideal customers are primarily IT project managers and similar roles at medium to large organizations.

She first wants to test her landing page for value. To do this she's going to offer two different pieces of content. One is designed to speak to her buyer's fear of IT audits, and the second focuses on the more positive side about being prepared for acquisitions by planning your IT strategy. She's curious which content connects the most with her audience.

The results from the first test showed that the consequences of being audited drove her buyers to engage the most. Elizabeth now wants to test to variations of the layout of the landing page to see which can communicate the value of her content piece the most. She offers the same audit strategy document on two different landing pages. The first page is the one she used in her first test, and the second is rearranged to highlight the consequences of IT audits and brings the form completely above the fold of the page.

Elizabeth found that the challenger page in her layout test improved the conversions for the strategy guide dramatically. She next wants to see if increasing the credibility of her organization might improve the results even further. Elizabeth decides to test two different variants of this against her previous test's winner. She doesn't have enough traffic on the page to test all three at a time, so she's going to pause the previous winner and try both variations at the same time. One version adds copy to the headline of the document stating that the content available in the guide was recently presented at a prominent industry conference. The second credibility test adds a small graphic to the layout showing that the content was featured in an article in a well-known trade publication.

Results for the recent credibility tests came back with mediocre results. There was some improvement, but when Elizabeth put the numbers into a statistical significance calculator, they didn't pass. She decides to move on in the hierarchy but notes that it's potentially worth coming back to this step later to try combining both the headline and magazine changes into a single challenger.

To test for social proof improvements, Elizabeth has a challenger page created that is almost the same of the earlier layout winner with one variation. In the new version, a picture of a happy customer with a quote

Brian Massey, Managing partner, Conversion Sciences, "The Conversion Scientist"

about how glad they are that they were prepared in advance for an audit.

Trust: The final step on the hierarchy is to test elements that back your company's ability to be trusted in the moment. When it comes to completing forms on a site, everyone is wondering if they'll get spammed, harassed by a sales rep, or even have their information sold to third parties. Addressing these concerns in the form can have impact, as well as "borrowing trust" from vendors by utilizing and displaying the logo of an encryption vendor. Enabling your marketing assets with SSL security has become table stakes for modern marketing.

HOW TO CONDUCT A MARKETING TEST

With an understanding of the different elements than can be tested in marketing, it's time to create a quick plan to make it happen!

STEP ONE: Determine your goal.

Make sure you're not testing for testing's sake! Do you want to increase engagement with your nurture emails or conversions on your content landing pages? Whatever your goal is, make sure you have one. This will keep your effort focused and ensure you the best chances at a positive outcome!

STEP TWO: Create a hypothesis.

Put on those lab coats, and think back to your high school science classes. A hypothesis is a best guess or hunch that if you make a change in your marketing, you'll get a positive increase in the result you want from your goal. The hierarchy of marketing optimization is where you go to come up with your testing ideas.

STEP THREE: Create your alternatives.

Using your ideas from the hypothesis, create one or more alternatives to what you're currently doing. Along with the original asset, these will serve as the test subjects. Don't feel like you need to make multiple alternatives. The more you create for any given test, the more time and traffic each will need. Less is definitely more!

STEP FOUR: Confirm your measurement.

With our creative energies fully engaged, we'll want to make sure our tools are set up to be able to measure our tests. Make sure you can measure the change in performance specifically for the goal you stated in step one!

STEP FIVE: Execute your test!

It's go time! With all of the preparation done, it's time to begin testing your alternatives with live traffic. This will often be done in A/B or multivariate testing fashion. It's important to know the difference between the two and pick the most appropriate one for your testing goal.

In our earlier example, Elizabeth tested multiple ideas as she progressed along the testing hierarchy. Each time, she was intentional with her test and the desired outcome. Let's dive into one specific test to see how she planned it long before A and B pages went live.

Elizabeth's goal was to engage more of her buyers with her content. This would result in an increase in both leads as well as creating more educated buyers. By being more informed, she hoped they would be of higher quality to sales.

In her first test, Elizabeth wanted to test for value. Her hypothesis was that tying her landing page copy and offers into strong emotions, she could connect with more of the site's visitors and more of them would convert on the landing page.

Her alternatives in the value test were certainly strong and contrasting offers. One spoke to the negative repercussions of an IT audit and the fear that it could happen at any time. The other offer promoted a more positive and proactive piece of content that addressed the benefits of IT being prepared for an organization's acquisitions and mergers.

Elizabeth's measurements for this test were the number of form completions, or conversions, each landing page had.

Elizabeth chose an A/B test for this first optimization. She would boost the traffic to the landing page with ads, emails, and more prominent banners, but it wouldn't have enough volume to test more than two alternatives at once.

A/B Testing

This is the most popular testing method due to its simplicity and lower level of test volume needed to get to a good result. Just like its name, A/B testing is simply testing two versions against each other, option A vs. option B, in a marketing optimization death match. Option A is most often your existing asset, landing page, or email template. This allows you to test a potentially better alternative against what is currently live. The benefit of testing in this fashion ensures you don't accidentally abandon a decent asset in the pursuit of two worse ones!

It's best practice when creating an A/B test to only change one element on option B from option A so that if you have a winner, you know what change made the difference.

Multivariate Testing

Multivariate testing is similar to A/B testing but allows you to test multiple subjects and multiple elements on each subject. It often looks like A vs. B vs. C vs. D. Large organizations with high volumes of traffic are needed for these tests.

A/B TESTING	MULTIVARIATE TESTING
Compare one major change at a time	Compare multiple changes at the same time
Quick to set up and test	Longer setup
Requires standard volumes	Requires much higher volumes
Pardot: Email Testing	Pardot: Landing Page Testing

A SIGNIFICANT TESTING TRAP

Before opening the floodgates of marketing optimization at your organization, it's important to understand the major testing trap that has tricked many a marketer!

When it comes to testing, the most important concept you need to be aware of is **statistical significance**. If you google this term, you'll get a very unfriendly looking mathematical definition. I can summarize it like this: *you want to make sure the results you get in your marketing testing are actually real and not just random chance.*

The risks of making decisions that aren't significant are that you'll waste time and money rebuilding and deploying results that you incorrectly think are successful across your marketing. It creates lots of busywork for a marketing team without any improved results.

The risks of making decisions that aren't significant are that you'll waste time and money rebuilding and deploying results that you incorrectly think are successful across your marketing.

You tested an email sent to a hundred people, and you had two versions: email A and email B. Email A got forty-nine clicks, and email B got fifty-one clicks. Is email B better? It's a trick question. Based on statistics, B is not technically better. The margin of error and some other statistics state that they're basically the same.

Brian Massey, Managing partner, Conversion Sciences, "Marketing Experiments"

We're trying to eliminate the possibility that we're simply flipping a coin with our marketing. There are two important concepts that come into play with statistically significant results: **sample size** and **effect size**.

Sample size refers to the volume of your test. How many total participants will there be? This could be the visitors to the landing page, recipients of the email test, or even prospects in the funnel.

Effect size refers to the difference between the results from each test. How many more conversions happened with the new landing page? The bigger the gap, the easier it is to tell that you have a significant answer, and only a small sample size is needed.

However, if the difference between results is small, you're going to need a much larger sample size to prove mathematically that you've found something statistically true. And many times, marketers don't have enough sample size for the small effect size, because their results are so tiny that they would need millions more clickers to test to see if it's significant. That means it's likely not, so move on. Test something higher on the hierarchy!

Empowered with a testing plan and the mathematical tools to prove your answers, there's nothing you can't do!

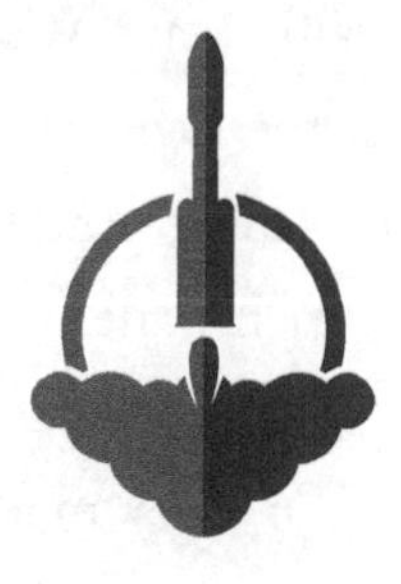

CHAPTER 11

PERSONALIZATION & DYNAMIC CONTENT

CSI Question Number Nine: Do you automatically change web or email content based on the recipient's segment?

A client of ours is in the health and life sciences vertical. They sell specifically to hospitals. First, I should point out that there's a big difference between public and private hospitals. For one, public hospitals are much larger. They're funded by local, state, and/or federal government budgets. They have many more beds, and because they receive public funding, they must take everyone who comes through the door. Private hospitals, on the other hand, are smaller in size, tend to be more selective about what insurance they take, and they can be more expensive. These smaller hospitals usually have better patient-to-doctor ratios.

Could you imagine talking to a staff member at both of these institutions in exactly the same way? What would happen? If you bring up a pain point about the logistics of so many beds, you just lost the attention of the private hospitals. Likewise, if you spoke on how to compassionately turn patients away, you lost the public hospitals.

So what did our client do? They made their website and email content change based on who was visiting their site, a private or a public hospital prospect. This is accomplished with a marketing automation feature called Advanced Dynamic Content. Setting it up on your homepage or landing page is a simple exercise for your web developer. They replace specific sections with a small bit of code that when loading, asks Pardot what should be displayed.

Once fully deployed and tagged appropriately, visitors experienced very specific messaging to their persona. It was pure magic.

If you were public hospital staff, in this case, you saw a public hospital image at the top of their website. The case studies and white papers that were offered on the site specifically mentioned public health in their titles. Likewise, if you were in private health, on the same website, you saw a private hospital case study, and the picture at the top was reminiscent of a private hospital. Once fully deployed and tagged appropriately, visitors experienced very specific messaging to their persona. It was pure magic.

The result of implementing advanced dynamic content for our healthcare client came in multiple ways:

- Landing page conversions shot up more than 120 percent. On the same page, both groups converted more, because to them it looked like a specific page.

- Email engagement increased by 30 percent simply by dynamically dropping public vs. private copy as well as specific hospital images in each message.
- Sales increased to the point where a new client shared that she had made the decision based on several factors, including the fact that our client had such a focus on public health.

Using advanced dynamic content in this situation drove a dramatic uptick in new leads that were created on the site and also increased the amount of engagement on existing buyers who downloaded and consumed more of the content. Why? It was specifically answering the challenges they had. A highlight was when a customer who purchased after experiencing the dynamic content shared with a sales rep that they were encouraged to choose their company because of its understanding of public health needs, which the company indeed did understand very well. There's magic when we speak to exactly who our buyers are.

Maura Rivera, VP of marketing, Qualified.com, "Conversational Marketing's Human Advantage"

As a best practice, you always have a default option that displays if you don't know the information you need in order to customize their experience. This can be whatever is currently in that section on your site. Note that if you display different images based on the industry of your visitors, you will need to first know what the industry of your visitor is before the automatic customization will take place.

There are vendors out there that address the unknown visitor. With Pardot and other marketing automation tools, you need your visitor to be an identified prospect for advanced dynamic content to kick in. This was why, in the example of the healthcare client, they sent an email to their list offering two different centers of excellence. With a single client on a Pardot tracked email, an anonymous visitor becomes a tracked prospect, and the ability to display custom content experiences is unlocked!

PERSONALIZATION

The feature highlighted in this chapter is one of the selling points on why many people buy marketing automation. It delivers on the promise of customizing the journey for the buyer, no matter what medium they're viewing, email or web.

Personalization: Designing or tailoring to meet an individual specification, need, or preference.

Personalization. What is it? It's a word with a lot of uses. The definition we're using means "designing or tailoring to meet an individual specification, need, or preference." Personalization is the art of speaking directly to your buyers using their words and challenges. Done right, it feels like you've singled them out of the crowd and understand them completely. The good news is that if you've been following this book's road map, personalization is built into almost every previous element of the CSI, starting with learning about our buyer personas in CSI number one from way back in chapter three.

We activated data based on buyers and segmentation in CSI number three (data preparedness), "Is your data clean, free of duplicates, and structured for reporting?" Then we built out specific content and pages, just as CSI number four (gated content marketing) instructed: "Do you use gated content to capture leads on your website?" Finally, we turned our attention to nurture campaigns, as is called for by CSI number five (multiple nurture campaigns), "Do you nurture your buyers in separate, relevant tracks?" You have been using personalization from the very beginning of this book!

GETTING & USING DATA

Back to the public and private hospital example. They had some great results, but there was some work that had to be done ahead of time, especially when it came to getting the data. At the start, they didn't have all the data for all of their buyers in their CRM and marketing automation tool. They knew that some accounts were private and some were public, based on the names of the respective companies, but the field we were using wasn't complete, and there were some gaps.

We worked with them to create an email that would be sent to all of their buyers offering them a link to one of two centers of excellence. The offer read something like, "We've created these two centers of knowledge and learning around both public and private health." There were two links in the email. One was to a webpage on their site talking all about references and resources concerning public health. The other link listed public and private resources on their site for private health and hospitals. Whichever link the client clicked on generally indicated their interest, and then we used Pardot to update their data fields. That's how we were able to fill in the gaps for the people we didn't know. For the few who still evaded us after

Randy Frisch, Cofounder and CMO, UberFlip, "Activating Content Marketing"

that, we added more questions on their forms so that when we first met new leads, we had additional data points to help us home in on their preferences right away.

Now it's time to use the data, but where can it go? Where are the different places you can use advanced dynamic content? Here are a few options that have always performed strongly for us.

The hero image on a website. A hero image is the main image on a webpage. It's often the large graphic on a homepage of a website at the very top, just underneath the navigation. This large image is usually one of the first things a visitor to your website sees, and if it makes sense to them, they're going to create a vision for your company based around this image. Oftentimes websites or successful companies will use pictures of their customers, their products, or the outcomes of their services.

Callouts in the sidebar. Often the margins of websites will contain callouts, or small boxes that offer something important to the visitor. "Hey, check out this white paper." "You might appreciate this case study." "Get a free trial today." They're almost like road advertisements on your website, and they're often in the margins. The whole side or even an individual callout could be outfitted with advanced dynamic content to show specific calls to action to visitors on your website.

Custom navigation. Your entire navigation on your website can be tailored to meet individual needs and preferences of your individual buyer personas.

Email headers. Similar to the hero image on a website, the large image at the beginning of a graphically designed email can be dynamically changed based upon the recipient of the email. This and other email changes often allow the marketer to create one email template to send to everyone and utilize advanced dynamic content to help personalize and customize the email to the recipient.

Email body and callouts. Different chunks of content—think whole paragraphs of text—can be altered inside your emails to speak specifically to your buyer. Many companies have done this at the top of the email in the introductory sentence or introductory paragraph to speak directly to their buyer. One successful customer used it to reference the local sports team. Another used it to localize various references, news, and weather reports at the very beginning of the email. They're able to send out one email and have it dynamically changed based on what they knew about their different segments.

Email and menu page calls to action. You can also change the call to action, the goal of the email, to match the specific buyer persona or segment that you're trying to target with advanced dynamic content.

Finally, **headlines and landing pages** can be changed to speak directly to those who are visiting. Crazy, right? The sky really is the limit. You'll need data for it, but once you get that in order, you're free to go crazy.

Once you activate advanced dynamic content, you'll see engage rates skyrocket. Leverage this activity to educate and nurture your buyers toward a faster purchase.

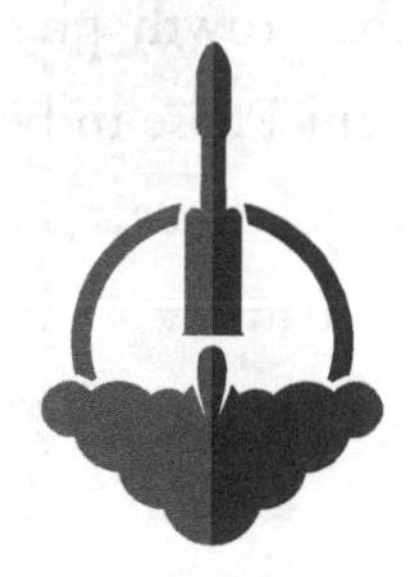

CHAPTER 12

MULTITOUCH ROI & ADVANCED REPORTING

CSI Question Number Ten: Do you know what marketing actions drive the most engagement and revenue?

Congratulations! You've reached the final element of the CSI, which includes the ever-popular and constantly evolving multi-touch reporting. Many marketers are either highly interested by the idea of this advanced reporting, or vague on what it exactly means. Sometimes both. As a result, many skip right to this step, only to realize that it is impossible to report on multiple touches when your marketing doesn't actually touch your buyers multiple times.

All of the work we've done throughout these chapters leads to this one. We need the data work from the Foundational Phase, the marketing touches from the growth phase, and the solid process with sales from the Alignment Phase to be able to find success with advanced reporting. But the good news is that if you put in the work along way through the CSI road map, multitouch reporting will be relatively straightforward to enact, and you'll have a gold mine of data to analyze.

CONSTRUCTION ZONE

No maturity model is complete without acknowledging the most advanced and cutting-edge strategies. While the rest of this book is grounded in proven marketing strategy that has been steadily delivering results for more than a decade, the topic of advanced analytics involves technology that is continually improving. The result is that any chapter on the technical side of multitouch analytics would be out of date the instant the words are written on the first draft. With this in mind, I want to focus on the strategies that should supersede all of the technology and should become easier and easier to execute as solutions evolve.

Andrew Krebs-Smith, CEO, Social Fulcrum, "Multi-Touch Attribution vs. Lift Study"

Recent acquisitions, such as those by Salesforce in the space of analytics and business intelligence, further highlight the need for grounded strategies amid the ever-innovating tech landscape. Anyone trying to follow and match their strategy with technical innovations experiences something like whiplash as capabilities constantly expand.

FIRST THINGS FIRST, REVISITED

In the Foundational Phase, we highlighted the importance of reporting, ROI, and understanding the source of leads. Capturing these "first touches" was intentionally placed early in the road map. Using marketing automation to identify the source of leads is straightforward and quick to implement and provides important intel on what marketing acquisition channels are performing the best.

Just as the placement of source ROI was deliberately early, the more advanced application of multitouch analytics was also intentionally placed in the last phase, the Optimization Phase. Until recently, technology for properly tracking beyond the first touch required extensive manual work or an entire separate system.

Some marketers are eager to implement a multitouch style of reporting as a way to justify their jobs in an organization. This is way more common than I'd like it to be, especially in organizations that are still evolving from a purely sales-driven model. ROI is not a bad thing; it is a great thing, actually. The first-touch ROI is early in the CSI, at number two. This should already be in place for your organization, and this first touch is what can earn you a seat at the table and help you justify your job if you need to. ROI allows you to show that you were able to use the money invested in marketing to create leads that turned into revenue for the company. But there are more touches that need to be explored and utilized to *keep* your seat at the table.

If you've followed the CSI road map, by the time you're implementing this chapter, you have all the ingredients available to get amazing details on what marketing actions drive the most revenue!

After all the hype and warnings, you might be wondering, "Just what the heck is multitouch reporting?" Before we go down the rabbit hole on the different ways you can do it, let's establish a working definition. To do that, let's consider our tenth CSI question: "Do you know what marketing actions drive the most engagement and revenue?" There is a simplicity in this challenge. We're going to be evaluating marketing actions with this reporting and connecting those actions to successful sales.

In first-touch attribution we evaluated the return on investment from various lead generation channels. In multitouch we shift from sources to measuring the effectiveness of every marketing (and often sales) actions across the entire buyer's journey. There is a subtle naming difference between these two that is important to draw distinctions. In fact, this little detail has led to many marketers getting both types of reporting wrong! It's important to clarify this.

A source is the way you acquired a lead, such as having met someone at a trade show. But when it comes to digital channels, a webinar itself isn't a source. Those who registered for your webinar had to find you first, and the way they did this is their actual source. So those who saw your webinar promoted on LinkedIn and clicked through should have LinkedIn listed as their source.

When marketers confuse source and touch, they can end up with source reports that include touches, which will end up not making much sense.

What is the webinar in this example? The webinar is the marketing action, touch, effort, or offer that attracted the prospect through that source. So our webinar goer has a lead source of LinkedIn, and the marketing action is the specific webinar.

The distinction is important because while we can often call lead source ROI reporting "first touch," it's a source rather than a touch. When marketers confuse source and touch, they can end up with source reports that include touches, which will end up not making much sense.

For example, if we had incorrectly labeled the webinar itself as the source and the ROI looks amazing, how do we get more leads like this? It doesn't make sense, because prospects didn't just magically come to our webinar. We had to promote the heck out of it. Anyone who has had a sparse attendance to a webinar that didn't get promoted can relate to this!

Conversely, if we properly attributed the way that prospects first found us and heard about our webinar, we can take real action on it. Let's say the stats show that we did get several attendees from promoting it on LinkedIn as well as many more from a paid ad on LinkedIn. If we're tracking both of those sources in marketing automation, we'll eventually be able to see if any of the ad spend converts to revenue.

Joseph Yelle, CEO, Analytics Cloud Consulting, "Analytics & AI Take Over the World"

In short, lead sources and that first touch is all about acquisition channels, and only those channels. The marketing offers associated with those sources and the subsequent marketing actions are then tracking specifically with multitouch.

ATTRIBUTION MODELING

Multitouch attribution is accomplished by first tracking the marketing actions that a buyer encounters and engages with. In Salesforce, for example, this is done by specifically tagging every buyer with a campaign for each action you want to track. The result of this work is that you have large amounts of data showing what marketing actions were a part of both buying processes, as well as those that didn't purchase.

With all of the activities tagged, you need a way to make sense of this information. This is done by weighting some or all of the touches based on how important they are to the buying process. The logic here is that not all marketing actions have equal impact on successfully moving the buyer forward.

There are many different kinds of weighting models that you can apply to your multitouch data. While I will cover each briefly, it's important to understand that this is where the gray area of multitouch reporting begins. Even assuming you tracked each and every marketing and sales action along the buying process, the weighting is the tricky part. By weighting, we're talking about giving credit to each action as a part of the successful sale.

Some strategists suggest that the type of activity should dictate how much credit an action gets. While most models try to simplify by giving credit based on *when* the action occurred. Let's review the most popular ones.

- **Linear multitouch model:** A perfect place to start, linear modeling gives equal credit to every touch point along the journey. I'm partial to this model because it eliminates user bias by weighting one touch over another. Over time and with enough data, the most effective touches should rise above the rest. The only drawback with a model like this is that it doesn't take key transitions of buyer stages into account. While you could argue that your awareness stage or decision to promote a lead to an MQL are arbitrary stages, it could be helpful to know what marketing action occurred right before the transition. Other models with shapes in their name attempt to capture this.

- **First-last (U-shaped) multitouch model:** This model emphasizes two key moments in a buyer journey. Often the moments are the first and last touch. The logic is that the first point, often something like the lead source, and the touch that occurred right before a purchase are the most important. When percentages are involved, you'll usually see both first and last touches receive 40 percent credit each. The remaining credit is often divided evenly on the touches in between. Note you could technically use this model to give importance to any two points. I've seen some weighting models give credit to the first touch as well as the touch that occurred right before a lead became an MQL and was sent to sales. While this has benefits, you miss out on all of the actions after the lead was sent to sales.
- **First-mid-last (W-shaped) multitouch model:** What is a W? It's a U with an extra point! This model highlights three key moments in type. Often these are the first touch, the transition to MQL, and the deal being closed. Many organizations that choose to weight based on timeline choose this model as it highlights the most important moments. It's more data crunching than the U shape, but not terribly overwhelming. Each action associated with a major transition or event gets roughly 22 percent of the credit. This does allow for the other actions to share the remaining 12 percent.
- **Custom modeling:** In case the previous models made attribution modeling appear too simple, many organizations take it a step further and customize their weighting model. Often they add more key moments to the mix, weight more to the

end of the sales cycle, or even weight specific actions based on information they have from buyer persona research. How fitting it is that buyer research work done on CSI number one should continue to be used across the CSI steps, including number ten!

Throughout this process, it's important to remember the goal of all of this work. We want to be able to identify what marketing actions drive the most engagement and ultimately revenue. To that end, many of the results from multitouch reporting are directional. This means that exact numerical measurements of a particular action may not be exact, but a collection of results may indicate a general direction to take.

> Throughout this process, it's important to remember the goal of all of this work. We want to be able to identify what marketing actions drive the most engagement and ultimately revenue.

I've seen this in action with our own multitouch reporting at Cheshire Impact. We have dashboards that show both individual actions and groups of marketing actions. It's amazing to see! One particular report shows the contribution of our webinars program. I do at least two webinars a month, each on a CSI topic. That is a considerable commitment of marketing time and effort so being able to see if they are impacting our revenue goals is important.

When reviewing one particular report, a webinar I did almost a year ago showed that it was associated with more revenue than any other webinar. I found this interesting as it wasn't a part of the main webinar program and was more of a seasonal topic. When we dove in deeper to the report, it was revealed that it occurred in a month with a lot of new clients, and our sales team had promoted the event to potential customers to encourage their sign-up.

Mathew Sweezey, Principal of Marketing Insights, Salesforce, "Preparing for the Context Revolution"

Without the context of why the webinar had performed so well, it wouldn't be outlandish for an organization to decide to do no webinars but the winning one. Instead, these metrics pointed to the importance of our webinar program for both top-of-funnel acquisition and reducing current customer churn.

MISSING THE GORILLA

When looking at directional data, it's important to keep your eyes open and not to focus too much on any particular data point. There's a famous basketball experiment by psychologists Christopher Chabris and Daniel Simons that comes to mind, an experiment that eventually led to them winning a Nobel Prize for psychology in 2004. A video shows two groups of people wearing different colored shirts, passing basketballs back and forth. Half the individuals are wearing white shirts, while the other half wears black. The goal of the person observing the experiment was to count the number of times the white team passes the ball back and forth, and to completely ignore the passes by the people in the black shirts. It sounded like a pretty decent experiment when I was shown this in a training once, and I was eager to get the number right. I remember viewing the video and dutifully focusing on the white team, counting their passes. One, two, three, four, five … the number went up, and I counted just those passes. It was very easy for me to completely ignore the other team.

After the video finished, we all shared our numbers out loud. "Great," said the facilitator of the training, "but did you see the gorilla?" During the video presentation, while we were watching the white team pass basketballs back and forth, a person in a gorilla suit literally walked out and waved at the camera. Not quickly. He sauntered out and waved at the camera. My classmates and I had been so focused on counting the white team's passes that we missed the freaking gorilla suit. This can happen with our data analysis too.

We can get too focused on a particular situation and not see what's actually happening around the data. That's why it's important to both test and consider the context of the results. Marketing is optimization. Utilize these strategies to increase the effectiveness of your campaigns!

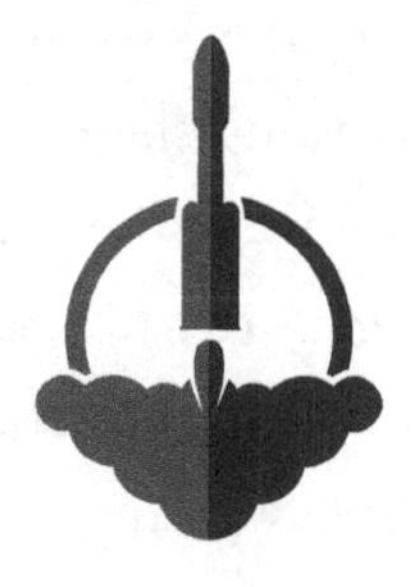

CHAPTER 13

GO TIME!

This book is full of success stories to inspire you on this awesome road of maximizing marketing automation. As this book draws to a close, I'd like to share one more of those success stories with you. It comes from an organization that has worked with Cheshire Impact since their implementation and that is doing amazing work with marketing automation.

They have experienced a 62 percent increase in new leads captured. They did it by using the techniques discussed in this book.

I know they're doing amazing work because it's been an absolute pleasure working with their marketing team and watching firsthand just how far they have come. Since enacting their marketing automation strategy, they have experienced a 62 percent increase in new leads captured. They did it by using the techniques discussed in this book, and guess what? It didn't require any additional spending on lead generation. Just by using these techniques and the visitors that were already present on their site, they began capturing more leads. Visitors were engaging more with their content, and as a result, they had a 267 percent increase in forms submissions. Driving those form submissions were people wanting to get more of the organization's content and additional information to contact them directly.

The concepts in this book are not a pipe dream. They're as reachable as these statistics, and right here waiting for you to grab hold. There are stats just like with our client above that are waiting to be achieved!

Now you have a goal: to maximize marketing automation and to help your company grow.

The CSI road map plans your strategy for you, one step at a time. I challenge you to do each step fully, because when you do, you will experience a snowball effect of compounding results.

Remember that simple definition we had for *strategy*: to have a goal and to create a plan to get there. Now you have a goal: to maximize marketing automation and to help your company grow. You also have goals for each step of the CSI, as well as strategies for getting there. Now it's time to execute!

Help Is a Click Away

There's nothing quite like a strategy book to inspire and overwhelm. I've been there and can completely relate. The good news is that you don't need to innovate and build in isolation. I've been fortunate enough to work with some of the best marketers in the business at Cheshire Impact. Their successes have been highlighted in many of the preceding chapters, and their support has been critical to the success of this book. I'd love to introduce you to the team! There are three main ways the team has supported massive marketing improvements in the organizations we work with:

- Strategy: Utilizing the same CSI framework you've just learned about, the team at Cheshire has strategic workshops, templates, and tools on every step! We provide strategic direction on maximizing both Pardot and Salesforce.
- Process: One of our most popular services maps out the entire marketing and sales processes, identifying the gaps and designing an optimized system flow.
- Technology: From initial implementations to executing marketing campaigns, the Cheshire team supports busy marketers by being the outsourced execution team with Pardot and Salesforce.
- For more information on how Cheshire Impact can help you reach your goals, visit us here and reach out: cheshireimpact.com/book

Final Note: Don't Be a Stranger

This is my first book. The creation process has been both amazing and challenging. I've noticed that many authors write from distant ivory towers. They're often equally as brilliant as they are inaccessible. While everyone has their own reasons, I prefer to be actively involved in the challenges, strategies, and career growth of marketers.

I'd love to hear from you! Email me anytime:
casey@cheshireimpact.com.

That's a wrap. The journey is yours. Enjoy each and every step. Onward and upward!

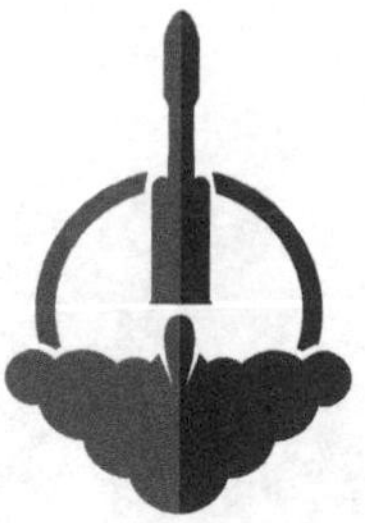

ABOUT THE AUTHOR

Casey is the founder and CMO of Cheshire Impact, the most experienced Salesforce Pardot consulting partner. A Marine Corps veteran, he is also the creator and host of the podcast *The Hard Corps Marketing Show*. As a marketing thought leader and marketing automation strategist, Casey has shared his craft with thousands of marketers at conferences across several continents. When not traveling, Casey enjoys spending time with his family, climbing tall mountains, and occasionally jumping out of perfectly good airplanes.

ACKNOWLEDGMENTS

I have learned a lot in the course of writing my first book, and the biggest lesson is that it's a team effort. Thank you to everyone who helped me see this through to its final form.

Thank you to all that helped with the project: Brian, Kim, Christina, Jennifer, Susan, Liane, Marissa, Nate, Peter, and Sophie. And to everyone at Team Chesh: Ann, Ayrielle, Daniel, David, Eri, Grayson, Issa, Jimmy, Katy, Leo, Logan, Malcolm, Ryan, Stephan, Steve, and Tim.

Printed in the USA
CPSIA information can be obtained
at www.ICGtesting.com
JSHW011114150224
57440JS00014B/65